ADA CARTIANU

COMPARATIVE ANALYSIS OF POLITICAL SYSTEMS
IN EUROPE AND THE UNITED STATES

BRIDGING THE ATLANTIC

AN OVERVIEW OF EUROPEAN AND U.S
POLITICAL LANDSCAPES

BRIDGING THE ATLANTIC
AN OVERVIEW OF EUROPEAN AND U.S POLITICAL LANDSCAPES
COMPARATIVE ANALYSIS OF POLITICAL SYSTEMS IN EUROPE AND THE UNITED STATES

TABLE OF CONTENTS

INTRODUCTION

Beyond the Shores:
A Philosophical Bridge Across the Atlantic

The vast expanse of the Atlantic Ocean, a historical highway and often perceived divider, whispers tales of intertwined destinies. For centuries, its watery depths have witnessed the ebb and flow of ideas, the migration of peoples, and the turbulent currents of political evolution that have shaped both the United States and the European Union. This book, "Bridging the Atlantic," is not merely a study of political science; it is an invitation to embark on a philosophical journey, one that demands a profound understanding of the multifaceted evolutions of political systems, the critical examination of underlying doctrines, and, ultimately, the cultivation of a shared sense of humanity.

The urgency of this endeavor stems from a fundamental reality: our world is increasingly interconnected. The challenges we face — climate change, pandemics, economic inequality — refuse to be confined by national borders. They are global in scope, demanding global solutions. In this context, understanding the political landscape of the US and the EU, two powerhouses that wield immense influence, is not simply an academic exercise, but a crucial step towards building a more just and sustainable future. To navigate the complexities of this future, we must delve into the histories, ideologies, and institutional architectures that have shaped these political entities.

The narratives of the US and the EU are distinct, yet interwoven with thoughts of shared ideals and contrasting experiences. From the nascent experiment of American democracy, forged in the crucible of revolution and shaped by ideals of individual liberty, to the gradual, often painstaking, integration of European nations, scarred by centuries of conflict and driven by a desire for unity, both have evolved in response to internal pressures and external forces. Understanding these evolutions requires a critical engagement with the core doctrines that underpin them: the individualistic ethos of American liberalism, the emphasis on social solidarity within European social democracies, the principles of federalism and subsidiarity that guide the EU's structure. We must not shy away from examining the inherent contradictions and limitations within these doctrines, the ways in which they have been used to both empower and oppress, to build and to divide.

However, knowledge without purpose is a sterile pursuit. The ultimate aim of understanding these political systems is not merely to dissect their mechanics, but to leverage this understanding to build a better world, a world characterized by inclusivity, diversity, acceptance, and, above all, love. These are not simply abstract ideals; they are the cornerstones of a society that values the dignity of every individual, regardless of their background, beliefs, or circumstances. This requires a conscious effort to dismantle the systems of oppression and exclusion that persist in both the US and the EU, legacies of colonialism, slavery, and discrimination. It demands a commitment to promoting policies that address inequality, protect vulnerable populations, and ensure that everyone has the opportunity to thrive.

The key to unlocking this potential lies in cultivating a sense of shared humanity. In an age of increasing polarization and fragmentation, it is easy to lose sight of the common ground that binds us together. We must resist the temptation to demonize those who hold different views, and instead strive to understand their perspectives, their fears, and their hopes. We must recognize that despite our differences, we are all members of a global community, bound by a shared destiny. Our fates are intertwined, and our collective survival depends on our ability to cooperate and collaborate.

This book, "Bridging the Atlantic," offers a roadmap for this vital journey. It invites us to move beyond the shores of national identity and embrace a broader vision of global citizenship. It challenges us to critically examine the doctrines that shape our world, to learn from the successes and failures of the past, and to forge a new path forward, one that is guided by the principles of justice, equality, and compassion.

In conclusion, bridging the Atlantic is not simply a matter of geographical proximity or political alliance. It is a philosophical endeavor, a commitment to understanding, empathy, and action. By embracing the lessons learned from the evolution of political systems in the EU and the US, by critically examining the doctrines that shape our world, and by cultivating a sense of shared humanity, we can forge a future defined by inclusivity, diversity, acceptance, and love. This is the challenge that lies before us, and it is one that we must embrace with courage, conviction, and unwavering hope. Only then can we truly shape a better world for ourselves and for generations to come.

SOVEREIGNTY IN DISCOURSE FEDERALISM VS. DECENTRALIZATION ACROSS THE ATLANTIC

INTRODUCTION TO SOVEREIGNTY IN DISCOURSE

Overview *of* Federalism *and* Decentralization

Federalism and decentralization are two governance frameworks that shape political organization and the distribution of power within states, particularly in the context of the United States and the European Union. Federalism typically involves a constitutional division of powers between a central authority and regional entities, allowing for a degree of autonomy among the latter. This division is often enshrined in a written constitution that outlines the specific jurisdictions of each level of government, ensuring a balance that prevents either the central government or the regional entities from becoming overly dominant. In contrast, decentralization refers to the transfer of authority and responsibility from central governments to local or regional governments, which may or may not be constitutionally enshrined. This transfer can take various forms, including devolution (where powers are granted to sub-national entities but can be revoked), delegation (where specific tasks are assigned to sub-national entities without transferring ultimate authority), and fiscal decentralization (where sub-national entities are given greater control over their own budgets). While both systems aim to enhance local governance and responsiveness, their implications for policy-making, national identity, and immigration are distinct, leading to different outcomes in the American and European contexts. The key difference lies in the inherent permanence and constitutional protection afforded to regional powers under federalism, compared to the more flexible and potentially reversible nature of decentralization.

In the United States, federalism is enshrined in the Constitution, which delineates the powers of the federal government and the states. The Tenth Amendment reserves powers not delegated to the federal government, nor prohibited to the states, to the states respectively, or to the people. This structure facilitates a balancing act where states can enact diverse immigration policies that reflect their regional values and demographics. For instance, states like California have adopted more inclusive immigration policies, offering in-state tuition to undocumented students and providing sanctuary protections, while others, such as Arizona, have pursued stricter measures, like enacting controversial laws aimed at deterring undocumented immigration. This variance underscores the complex interplay between federal mandates and state autonomy, revealing how federalism can both empower and complicate immigration governance. The federal government maintains control over naturalization and border security, while states handle aspects like education, healthcare, and law enforcement, which significantly affect immigrant communities. The resulting patchwork of policies also raises questions about national identity, as differing state approaches can lead to conflicting perceptions of what it means to be American. A Californian with a welcoming perspective on immigration might have a vastly different understanding of national identity compared to someone in a state with more restrictive immigration policies. These discrepancies can contribute to political polarization and challenges in achieving comprehensive immigration reform at the federal level.

In Europe, the situation is further complicated by the EU's supranational framework, which introduces an additional layer of governance that influences national policies. The EU operates on the principle of subsidiarity, meaning that decisions are taken at the lowest possible level of governance, but the EU also possesses considerable authority in areas like trade, competition, and immigration. Member states retain significant control over their immigration policies, reflecting their diverse histories, cultures, and economic needs, but EU regulations often set minimum standards that shape national practices. For example, the Dublin Regulation dictates which member state is responsible for examining an asylum application, and the Schengen Area allows for passport-free travel between many EU countries, impacting border control and immigration flows. This duality of governance raises critical questions regarding sovereignty and identity, particularly as countries grapple with the challenges of immigration in a multicultural context. The rise of nationalist movements across Europe underscores the tension between national identity and the supranational identity promoted by the EU. Decentralization seen in some European nations, such as Spain with its autonomous communities, allows regional governments to adapt their policies to local needs, but it can also lead to tensions with national directives and EU regulations, complicating the broader European project of integration. For instance, Catalonia's pursuit of greater autonomy has included disagreements over immigration policy, reflecting the complexities of balancing regional identity with national and European frameworks.

Cultural influences play a crucial role in the dynamics of federalism and decentralization, shaping how regions approach immigration and identity. In the U.S., regional beliefs about immigration often reflect historical narratives, economic conditions, and demographic changes, leading to varied public opinions across states. States with a history of welcoming immigrants, such as New York and California, tend to have more positive views on immigration, while those with a history of economic hardship or demographic shifts may harbor more anxieties. Economically, states that rely on immigrant labor in agriculture or manufacturing may have more pragmatic views on immigration reform, while states with declining industries may view immigration as a threat to jobs. These variations are reflected in state-level policies and political discourse. Similarly, in Europe, cultural attitudes towards immigration are influenced by historical experiences, such as colonial legacies and post-war migration patterns. Countries like France and the United Kingdom, with their colonial past, have diverse populations as a result of immigration from former colonies, leading to complex debates about integration and national identity. Post-war migration patterns, particularly the arrival of guest workers in countries like Germany, have also shaped cultural attitudes towards immigration. These cultural contexts inform political discourse and public opinion, affecting how immigration policies are crafted and implemented at both the regional and national levels. The rise of anti-immigrant sentiment in some European countries highlights the challenges of integrating diverse populations and preserving national identity in an era of globalization.

The relationship between federalism, decentralization, and immigration policy highlights the complexities of governance in contemporary societies. The challenges of managing migration flows, integrating diverse populations, and addressing security concerns require innovative and adaptable approaches. The differences between the U.S. and EU models showcase how varying approaches to power distribution can influence national identity, economic conditions, and public sentiment. The U.S. federal system provides a framework for states to experiment with different immigration policies, but it also creates a patchwork of laws that can be confusing and inefficient. The EU's supranational framework aims to harmonize immigration policies across member states, but it faces resistance from countries that prioritize national sovereignty. As both regions continue to navigate the challenges of immigration in an increasingly interconnected world, understanding the nuances of federalism and decentralization becomes essential for policymakers and scholars alike. Comparing policy outcomes and public perceptions in different federal and decentralized systems can offer valuable insights on how to design more effective and equitable immigration policies. This comparative analysis not only enriches the discourse on sovereignty but also illuminates the lessons that can be drawn from each approach in addressing the multifaceted issues surrounding immigration and identity. Further research is needed to explore the long-term effects of different governance models on immigrant integration, social cohesion, and economic prosperity. Ultimately, a nuanced understanding of the interplay between federalism, decentralization, and immigration policy is crucial for building more inclusive and resilient societies in both the United States and Europe.

THE IMPORTANCE OF TRANSATLANTIC PERSPECTIVES

Federalism, Decentralization, *and the* Shaping of Governance

The significance of transatlantic perspectives in the discourse surrounding federalism and decentralization cannot be overstated. This dialogue offers a unique and invaluable lens through which to examine the complexities of governance, particularly in light of the diverse and often contrasting approaches to immigration policy and the construction of national identity. Both the United States and the European Union grapple with the fundamental tension between central authority and regional autonomy, yet they frequently arrive at divergent conclusions rooted in their distinct historical contexts, deeply ingrained cultural values, and evolving political landscapes. By rigorously exploring these transatlantic perspectives, scholars, policymakers, and engaged citizens alike can gain a more nuanced and comprehensive understanding of how federal and decentralized systems function in practice, and how these systems impact pressing social and economic issues.

Transatlantic comparisons provide critical and often illuminating insights into how immigration policies are shaped by federal versus decentralized governance structures. In the United States, immigration is largely managed at the federal level, resulting in a uniform policy framework intended to apply across the nation. However, this centralized approach often clashes with the diverse local realities faced by individual states and municipalities, leading to friction and debate over resource allocation, enforcement, and integration strategies. Conversely, many European nations adopt a more decentralized approach to immigration, empowering regional governments to play a significant role in shaping policies that address local needs and circumstances. This fundamental difference in approach influences not only how immigrants are integrated into society, affecting their access to services, employment opportunities, and social support networks, but also how national identity is constructed and negotiated, leading to varying levels of inclusivity and social cohesion. A comprehensive analysis of these divergent practices reveals the profound implications for social cohesion, economic development, and public perception of immigrants in both contexts.

Cultural influences play a pivotal and often underestimated role in the ongoing debate over federalism and decentralization. In the United States, the traditional concept of a "melting pot" reflects a historical narrative that promotes assimilation into a singular, overarching national identity. This ideal, while historically influential, is increasingly challenged by perspectives that emphasize diversity and multiculturalism. In contrast, many European countries have embraced, to varying degrees, the concept of multiculturalism, leading to more localized and context-specific approaches to governance and immigration. This divergence highlights how borders and beliefs intersect, shaping political discourse and public opinion on immigration. Understanding these cultural underpinnings is essential for addressing the complex challenges that arise in both regions, particularly as they navigate the ever-increasing complexities of globalization, demographic shifts, and the rise of nationalist sentiments.

The role of regional governments in shaping immigration policies further illustrates the critical importance of examining transatlantic perspectives. In the United States, states like California and Texas, with their significant immigrant populations and distinct political climates, have adopted divergent approaches to immigration, often reflecting the deeply held values and beliefs of their constituents. These state-level policies range from offering in-state tuition to undocumented students to enacting stringent enforcement measures. Similarly, in Europe, regional entities such as Catalonia in Spain and Flanders in Belgium assert their autonomy in immigration matters, advocating for policies that align with their unique cultural identities and economic priorities. By studying these case studies in detail, it becomes evident that the intricate interplay between federal and regional authorities significantly influences not only policy outcomes but also the broader societal attitudes toward immigration and integration.

Furthermore, the economic implications of federalism and decentralization cannot be overlooked in the context of immigration. Both the United States and the European Union face complex economic pressures that are often exacerbated by immigration trends, including debates over labor market competition, social welfare costs, and the contributions of immigrants to economic growth. However, their responses to these pressures often differ significantly based on their distinct governance structures. Federal systems, while aiming for national uniformity, may struggle to effectively address regional economic disparities and the varying needs of local economies. Conversely, decentralized systems, while potentially fostering innovation and localized solutions, may also lead to inconsistencies in policy and exacerbate inequalities between regions. A transatlantic perspective allows for a comparative analysis of these economic realities, offering valuable lessons and best practices that can inform future policy decisions and promote more equitable and sustainable economic outcomes.

Expanding beyond immigration, a transatlantic perspective also illuminates diverse approaches to other key areas of governance, such as environmental regulation, healthcare provision, and education policy. Examining how the EU and the US balance central mandates with regional autonomy in these sectors can reveal the strengths and weaknesses of each model, offering valuable insights for policymakers seeking to improve the effectiveness and responsiveness of their own systems. For example, comparing the EU's approach to environmental protection, with its emphasis on supranational regulations and coordinated action, to the US's more decentralized and often litigious system can shed light on different strategies for addressing climate change and other environmental challenges.

The importance of transatlantic perspectives lies in their ability to enrich and deepen the ongoing discourse on sovereignty, federalism, and decentralization, ultimately providing a more comprehensive and nuanced framework for understanding contemporary challenges in governance. By fostering dialogue and exchange between scholars, policymakers, and citizens on both sides of the Atlantic, we can learn from each other's experiences, identify best practices, and develop innovative solutions to the complex challenges facing our societies in an increasingly interconnected world. This collaborative approach is essential for building more resilient, equitable, and democratic societies that are capable of addressing the challenges of the 21st century. The exploration of transatlantic perspectives is not merely an academic exercise; it is a crucial tool for shaping a more just and prosperous future for all.

FEDERALISM AND DECENTRALIZATION HISTORICAL PERSPECTIVES

Evolution *of* Federal Systems *in the* U.S

Decentralization, multilevel governance, and federalism are closely related terms that all address the organization of the public sector across different levels or administrative tiers. However, the term 'federalism' denotes a specific type of vertical governance arrangement. While unitary (non-federal) countries can choose to pursue a wide variety of decentralization reforms, decentralization and multilevel governance are, by definition, important features of federal countries. So, what exactly is federalism?

Federalism is a governance system of self-rule and shared rule. In other words, governance powers are divided and shared between a general government having certain nationwide, continent-wide, or worldwide responsibilities and regional governments with regional powers. This division of powers is combined with the authority to carry out those responsibilities on behalf of the people of the federal body.

The word "federal" comes from the Latin *foedus,* which means covenant or treaty. The Federal idea or covenant (agreement) signifies a binding governance partnership among co-equals in which the parties retain their individual identity and integrity while creating a new entity in the body politic that has its own identity and integrity. This delicate balance between unity and autonomy is the defining characteristic of federalism, and its successful implementation requires constant negotiation and adaptation.

The evolution of federal systems in the United States reflects a complex interplay of historical contexts, political ideologies, and social movements that have shaped the nation's governance. The foundation of American federalism was established in the late 18th century with the ratification of the Constitution, which created a division of powers between the national and state governments. This structure aimed to balance the need for a strong central authority with the desire for local autonomy, ensuring that states retained significant powers to govern themselves. The enumeration of specific powers to the federal government in Article I, Section 8 of the Constitution, such as the power to declare war and regulate interstate commerce, was carefully crafted to prevent the overreach of federal authority. Conversely, the Tenth Amendment reserved powers not delegated to the federal government, nor prohibited to the states, to the states respectively, or to the people. Over time, this carefully constructed framework has been tested and transformed by various challenges, including civil rights movements, economic crises, and shifting demographics, each influencing the dynamics between federal and state authorities. These challenges have often revealed inherent tensions within the system and spurred debates about the appropriate balance of power.

The early years of the American republic were marked by significant debates regarding the proper scope of federal power. The Federalist and Anti-Federalist factions held contrasting views, with the Federalists advocating for a stronger national government to ensure stability and promote economic growth, while the Anti-Federalists championed states' rights and feared the potential for federal tyranny. The Whiskey Rebellion, for example, demonstrated the federal government's willingness to assert its authority in matters of taxation, but also highlighted the potential for conflict when federal policies clashed with local interests. The Marshall Court, under Chief Justice John Marshall, played a crucial role in strengthening the federal government through landmark decisions that broadly interpreted the Necessary and Proper Clause and affirmed the supremacy of federal law. These early interpretations laid the groundwork for the gradual expansion of federal power that would characterize much of the 19th and 20th centuries.

The Civil War marked a pivotal moment in the evolution of federalism, as it raised fundamental questions about the nature of sovereignty and the limits of state authority. The conflict was, at its core, a struggle over the balance of power between the federal government and individual states, particularly concerning the institution of slavery. The Confederate states asserted their right to secede from the Union, claiming that their sovereignty superseded federal authority. The Union victory ultimately affirmed the indivisibility of the nation and the supremacy of federal law. The aftermath of the war led to the Reconstruction era, during which the federal government asserted its dominance in enforcing civil rights and integrating formerly enslaved individuals into society. This period solidified the federal government's role in protecting individual rights, thus expanding its influence over states. The subsequent amendments to the Constitution, particularly the Fourteenth and Fifteenth Amendments, not only altered the balance of power but also set a precedent for future federal intervention in state matters, especially concerning social justice and economic regulation. These amendments laid the legal foundation for the Civil Rights Movement of the 20th century and empowered the federal government to challenge discriminatory state laws and practices.

The 20th century brought about significant changes in American federalism, particularly during the New Deal era. The economic turmoil of the Great Depression prompted the federal government to take unprecedented actions to stabilize the economy, expanding its role in public welfare and economic management. President Franklin D. Roosevelt's New Deal programs, such as Social Security and the Works Progress Administration, represented a dramatic expansion of the federal government's role in providing social safety nets and regulating the economy. This shift marked a departure from the more limited federal government envisioned by the Founding Fathers and illustrated how crises can catalyze the evolution of federal systems. The establishment of various federal agencies and programs underscored the necessity of a centralized approach to address national challenges, reshaping the relationship between federal and state governments. While these programs were widely credited with alleviating the suffering caused by the Depression, they also sparked debates about the appropriate balance between federal and state authority, with some critics arguing that the New Deal represented an overreach of federal power.

In recent decades, the rise of globalization and increased immigration have further influenced the evolution of federal systems in the U.S. Globalization has led to increased interconnectedness and interdependence, requiring greater coordination between countries on issues such as trade, security, and environmental protection. This has, in turn, placed new demands on the federal government to negotiate and enforce international agreements, sometimes at the expense of state autonomy. The challenges posed by immigration policy have necessitated a reevaluation of how federal and state governments interact, particularly regarding the integration of newcomers and the preservation of national identity. The federal government holds primary responsibility for setting immigration policy and enforcing immigration laws, but states bear the brunt of providing services to immigrants, such as education, healthcare, and social welfare. States have often taken the lead in crafting their own immigration policies, sometimes in direct opposition to federal directives. This phenomenon highlights the tensions inherent in a federal system, where local beliefs and cultural influences can drive divergent approaches to governance, reflecting the broader question of how sovereignty is negotiated in a multicultural society. Sanctuary cities, for example, represent a clear assertion of local autonomy in the face of federal immigration policies.

Furthermore, the information age and the rise of digital technologies have presented new challenges to the balance of power between the federal government and the states. Issues such as data privacy, cybersecurity, and internet regulation require novel approaches that often transcend traditional jurisdictional boundaries. The federal government has sought to assert its authority in these areas, but states have also been active in developing their own regulations and standards. This has led to a complex and sometimes conflicting landscape of laws and regulations, highlighting the need for greater coordination and cooperation between the federal government and the states.

As the U.S. continues to grapple with issues of federalism and decentralization, the ongoing discourse reflects the challenges of maintaining a cohesive national identity while respecting regional differences. The evolution of federal systems is not merely a historical narrative; it is an ongoing dialogue about the role of government in addressing the complexities of modern society. This discourse is particularly salient in the context of immigration policy, environmental regulations, and healthcare reform, where the intersection of federal authority and state autonomy will likely shape the future of American federalism. The lessons learned from this evolution offer valuable insights into the broader comparative analysis of federalism and decentralization, particularly in relation to transatlantic political dynamics and the ongoing debates about the appropriate level of governance for addressing global challenges. Studying the successes and failures of American federalism can provide valuable guidance for other countries seeking to navigate the complexities of balancing national unity with regional autonomy in an increasingly interconnected world.

DECENTRALIZATION:
A Multi-Level Governance Imperative

Central governments, local governments, and other territorial bodies operate within a complex web of interdependence, a reality that demands a shift in perspective regarding decentralization. No longer should these entities be viewed as isolated actors, but rather as crucial components of a multi-layered system designed to deliver effective public services and foster local development. This essay argues that the key to successful decentralization lies not in a simple 'decentralize or not' dichotomy, but in strategically assigning responsibilities, bolstering capacity, and fostering coordination across all levels of government, thereby empowering local stakeholders to enhance the efficiency, equity, and sustainability of public services.

The local public sector, operating at the nexus of residents, civil society, and the private sector, serves as the primary interface between the public and governmental institutions. It encompasses a diverse range of actors, from devolved local governments and deconcentrated local administrations to NGOs and parastatal organizations providing delegated services, as well as localized services delivered by central agencies. This sector is where citizens directly experience the benefits (or shortcomings) of public services, and it is within this space that the promise of decentralization must be realized.

The reality in most nations is a complex interplay of responsibilities, with various levels of government contributing to the provision of frontline services, often funded through a patchwork of intergovernmental mechanisms. This complexity necessitates a nuanced understanding of decentralization and local governance as a multi-level system. The effectiveness of local governments hinges on the institutional context within which they operate, a context shaped by the intricate relationships with higher levels of government. Therefore, focusing solely on the local level without considering the broader intergovernmental framework is a recipe for inefficiency and stunted development.

The critical question, then, is not whether decentralization is inherently good or bad, nor which specific model to blindly adopt. The true challenge lies in optimizing the allocation of functional responsibilities, improving the capabilities of stakeholders at all levels, and fostering seamless coordination. It's about empowering local governments and other local actors to drive improvements in public service delivery, ensure equitable distribution of resources, promote the long-term sustainability of public spending, and act as catalysts for a territorial approach to local development. This approach recognizes the unique characteristics and needs of each locality and tailors solutions accordingly, fostering a more responsive and effective form of governance.

Political decentralization plays a pivotal role in ensuring that citizens' voices are heard and represented in local decision-making processes. It is the bedrock of an effective, inclusive, and responsive system of local governance. By establishing elected local or regional governments, we introduce another layer of government that not only enhances political participation but also fosters a more competitive political landscape. More importantly, it creates a crucial vertical balance of power, holding those in power accountable to the people they serve. This accountability is paramount in preventing corruption, ensuring transparency, and ultimately delivering better outcomes for citizens.

While local political systems are inherently tied to specific national and contextual circumstances, certain key elements consistently contribute to their effectiveness, inclusivity, and responsiveness. The crucial link is that a local government can only be held politically accountable for fulfilling its responsibilities if it possesses the necessary autonomy and discretion to perform those functions effectively. In other words, accountability and empowerment must go hand in hand (World Bank, 2009).

Firstly, locally elected officials must be granted meaningful discretion, the genuine authority and decision-making power necessary to perform their functions in a way that reflects the preferences and priorities of the citizens they represent. This extends beyond merely transferring legal functional responsibilities. It also necessitates granting local leaders the power to direct local government staff and exercise control over allocated financial resources. Without this level of autonomy, local governments are merely implementing agents of central directives, unable to truly address the unique needs of their communities.

Secondly, political and electoral systems should be designed to incentivize locally elected leaders to prioritize the interests of their constituents, rather than pursuing personal gain or serving narrow political agendas. This requires establishing robust ethical codes, promoting transparency in campaign finance, and fostering a culture of public service. Electoral systems that encourage direct engagement with citizens and reward responsiveness to their concerns are crucial in ensuring that elected officials remain accountable to the people they represent.

Thirdly, effective public and social accountability mechanisms must be in place to enable local constituents and other relevant stakeholders to hold the local government and its elected officials responsible for their performance. This includes providing access to information, establishing channels for citizen feedback and complaint resolution, and empowering civil society organizations to monitor government activities and advocate for the public interest. Independent audits, investigative journalism, and robust citizen oversight committees are all essential components of a strong accountability framework.

Decentralization is not a simple act of transferring power; it is a complex and dynamic process of building a multi-layered system of governance that fosters collaboration, empowers local actors, and prioritizes the needs of citizens. By focusing on the strategic allocation of responsibilities, the enhancement of capacity at all levels, and the promotion of seamless coordination, we can unlock the true potential of decentralization to deliver more efficient, equitable, and sustainable public services, and to serve as a catalyst for inclusive territorial development. The key lies in recognizing the inherent interdependence of central and local governments and working together to build a more responsive and accountable system of governance that benefits all.

DEVELOPMENT OF DECENTRALIZATION IN EUROPE

A Multifaceted Evolution

The development of decentralization in Europe represents a complex and multifaceted evolution, deeply intertwined with the continent's historical syntheses, political ideologies, and evolving socio-economic realities. Tracing its trajectory requires an understanding of the diverse contexts that have shaped the political landscape, from the post-World War II era to the present, marked by the rise of the European Union and the challenges of globalization. In the aftermath of the devastating conflicts of the 20th century, many European nations embarked on a path of institutional reform, seeking to prevent the resurgence of totalitarian regimes and promote lasting stability. A key element of this strategy was the redistribution of power away from centralized authority, fostering a greater degree of autonomy and responsibility at regional and local levels.

This shift towards decentralized governance was driven by the recognition that centralized states often struggled to effectively address the unique needs and aspirations of diverse populations scattered across geographically and culturally distinct regions. The horrors of centralized control under fascist and communist regimes underscored the importance of empowering local communities and giving them a greater voice in shaping their own destinies. This gradual shift towards regional governance was not a uniform process, but rather a tailored approach that reflected the specific historical, social, and political circumstances of each nation.

The establishment of the European Union further accelerated the trend towards decentralization, albeit in a more nuanced and indirect manner. While the EU itself represents a supranational entity with its own centralized institutions, its emphasis on subsidiarity and its commitment to regional development have encouraged member states to adopt decentralized frameworks in governance. The principle of subsidiarity, enshrined in the Treaty on European Union, dictates that decisions should be taken at the lowest possible level of government, empowering regional and local authorities to address issues within their competence. Furthermore, the EU's regional policy, through initiatives like the European Regional Development Fund, provides financial support to regions across Europe, enabling them to invest in infrastructure, innovation, and economic development, thereby strengthening their capacity for self-governance. This promotion of regional autonomy has enhanced political pluralism, fostered a stronger sense of regional identity, and contributed to a more balanced distribution of power within European states.

The role of regional governments in shaping immigration policies has emerged as a particularly significant aspect of decentralization in Europe, reflecting the growing importance of local contexts in managing the challenges and opportunities associated with migration. As immigration patterns shifted and the influx of migrants transformed demographic landscapes, regional authorities found themselves on the front lines, grappling with the practical implications of integrating newcomers into their communities. This proximity to the ground allowed them to develop a nuanced understanding of the specific challenges faced by migrants and host communities alike, enabling them to craft localized policies that were more responsive and effective than top-down approaches dictated by national governments.

These localized policies often involved a combination of measures, including language training, job placement programs, and cultural integration initiatives designed to facilitate the successful integration of migrants into the social and economic fabric of the region. Moreover, regional governments have often played a crucial role in promoting intercultural dialogue and combating discrimination, fostering a more inclusive and welcoming environment for newcomers. In countries such as Spain and Italy, regional governments have leveraged their autonomy to implement innovative integration strategies, demonstrating how decentralization can enhance responsiveness to immigration-related issues while fostering a sense of local belonging. For instance, some regions have established dedicated offices to assist migrants in navigating the bureaucratic processes associated with residency permits and access to public services, while others have launched initiatives to promote entrepreneurship and self-employment among migrant communities.

However, the decentralization of immigration policies also presents challenges. Disparities in resources and capacity among different regions can lead to uneven levels of integration success, potentially creating pockets of social exclusion and resentment. Furthermore, the lack of coordination between regional and national authorities can result in conflicting policies and bureaucratic inefficiencies, hindering the overall effectiveness of immigration management. Therefore, a balanced approach is needed, one that recognizes the importance of regional autonomy while ensuring that national governments retain overall responsibility for setting immigration policy and coordinating integration efforts.

Moreover, the comparative analysis of federalism and decentralization in Europe reveals distinct approaches to governance and citizenship, each with its own strengths and weaknesses. While federal systems, such as that of Germany, maintain a constitutionally defined distribution of powers between national and regional governments, decentralized systems like those in Belgium exhibit a more fluid and negotiated interaction between various territorial entities. In federal systems, the division of powers is typically enshrined in a constitution, providing a clear framework for the relationship between the federal government and the constituent states. This can promote stability and predictability, ensuring that each level of government has a defined sphere of responsibility. However, it can also lead to rigidity and inflexibility, making it difficult to adapt to changing circumstances.

In contrast, decentralized systems often rely on a more flexible and negotiated approach, with powers being delegated to regional and local authorities through legislation or agreements. This allows for greater adaptability and responsiveness to local needs, but it can also create uncertainty and complexity, as the division of powers may be subject to ongoing negotiations and reinterpretations. This complexity often influences public opinion on national identity and immigration, as citizens navigate their affiliations within both regional and national frameworks. In federal systems, citizens may have a stronger sense of allegiance to their state or region, while in decentralized systems, the lines between regional and national identity may be more blurred.

The interaction between local autonomy and national cohesion raises critical questions about how societies can balance the rights of regional entities with overarching national interests. How can national governments ensure that regional policies are consistent with national goals, while respecting the autonomy and diversity of local communities? How can societies foster a sense of national unity and identity in the face of increasing regional diversity and autonomy? These are complex and challenging questions that require careful consideration and ongoing dialogue.

Cultural influences play a pivotal role in shaping the discourse surrounding federalism and decentralization in Europe. Historical legacies, linguistic diversity, and regional identities inform how different societies perceive the relationship between central authority and local governance. In regions with strong cultural identities, such as Catalonia in Spain or Flanders in Belgium, demands for greater autonomy often intertwine with immigration debates, as local populations grapple with notions of belonging and national identity. These cultural dimensions underscore the necessity of understanding decentralization not merely as a governance structure but as a reflection of the values and beliefs that underpin societal cohesion.

For instance, in regions with strong linguistic identities, the protection and promotion of the local language may be seen as a key element of regional autonomy. This can lead to tensions with national governments that may prioritize the use of a national language. Similarly, in regions with distinct cultural traditions, there may be resistance to immigration policies that are perceived as threatening the region's cultural identity. These cultural dimensions highlight the importance of finding a balance between respecting regional diversity and promoting national unity.

As Europe continues to navigate the complexities of decentralization, the economic implications of this governance model also warrant attention. Decentralization can enhance regional economic development by allowing local authorities to tailor policies that respond to specific economic contexts. For example, regional governments can implement targeted investment strategies to promote innovation and entrepreneurship in specific sectors, or they can develop customized training programs to meet the needs of local employers. However, it can also lead to disparities in resource allocation and investment, particularly in relation to immigration.

Regions that successfully integrate migrants into their economies can benefit from increased labor supply, innovation, and cultural diversity, while those that struggle may face social tensions and economic challenges. The availability of resources and infrastructure, the effectiveness of integration policies, and the level of social cohesion all play a role in determining whether immigration has a positive or negative impact on regional economies. Thus, the development of decentralization in Europe not only influences political structures but also significantly impacts the socio-economic fabric of the continent, shaping its future in an increasingly interconnected world. As Europe strives to balance the benefits of regional autonomy with the need for national cohesion and economic competitiveness, the evolution of decentralization will continue to be a defining feature of its political and social landscape. The key lies in fostering a collaborative approach that empowers regional authorities while ensuring that national governments retain the capacity to address overarching challenges and promote the well-being of all citizens.

KEY HISTORICAL EVENTS SHAPING CURRENT DISCOURSE

ON FEDERALISM, DECENTRALIZATION, AND IMMIGRATION

The discourse surrounding federalism and decentralization, particularly as it relates to immigration policies, is deeply rooted in historical events that have sculpted political landscapes on both sides of the Atlantic. These events have not only established precedents for the balance of power within federal systems but have also significantly influenced public opinion, policy outcomes, and the evolving concepts of national identity and sovereignty. From the American Civil War to the rise of globalization and the resurgence of populist movements, understanding these historical underpinnings is crucial for navigating the complexities of contemporary immigration debates.

One of the most formative events shaping the understanding of federalism in the United States was the American Civil War. This conflict, fought over issues of states' rights, primarily the right to maintain slavery, starkly illuminated the tensions inherent in a federal system. The war served as a crucible, forging a more centralized federal government and establishing the principle of national supremacy. The subsequent Reconstruction era, with its federal interventions in the Southern states to protect the rights of formerly enslaved people, further redefined the relationship between state sovereignty and national unity. This period witnessed the passage of landmark constitutional amendments, such as the 14th Amendment, which enshrined the principles of equal protection and due process under federal law. These principles continue to be invoked in contemporary debates surrounding immigration, particularly in cases involving discrimination and the rights of immigrants under federal and state laws. The legacy of the Civil War and Reconstruction informs contemporary debates about immigration policies and cultural identity by highlighting the ongoing tension between states' rights and the federal government's responsibility to ensure equal protection and uphold constitutional rights.

In Europe, the historical context of federalism and decentralization unfolds differently, primarily shaped by the devastating experience of World War II. The war underscored the dangers of unchecked nationalism and the urgent need for international cooperation. This realization led to the gradual establishment of the European Union, a unique experiment in supranational governance aimed at fostering cooperation, economic integration, and lasting peace among member states. The EU's creation represented a significant shift towards decentralization of certain powers to a supranational body, while simultaneously emphasizing the importance of regional identities within member states. This delicate balance between national sovereignty and shared governance has profoundly impacted immigration policies. The Schengen Area, which allows for free movement of people across borders, exemplifies this tension. While it has facilitated economic integration and cultural exchange, it has also raised concerns about border security and the potential strain on social welfare systems, leading to complex negotiations and compromises among member states regarding immigration policies. The historical context of European integration provides a backdrop for analyzing how federalism and decentralization can coexist in addressing modern challenges, particularly those related to immigration, border control, and cultural integration.

The late 20th century witnessed the accelerating force of globalization, further complicating the debates surrounding federalism, decentralization, and immigration. As nations became increasingly interconnected through trade, technology, and migration, traditional notions of national identity and sovereignty were challenged. The movement of people across borders intensified, leading to both economic opportunities and social anxieties. In the United States, this phenomenon fueled debates over immigration reform, border security, and the role of states in regulating immigration. States with large immigrant populations, such as California, Texas, and Florida, have developed diverse and often conflicting approaches to immigration policy, reflecting their unique demographics, economic needs, and political climates. Some states have embraced more welcoming policies, offering sanctuary to undocumented immigrants, while others have adopted stricter enforcement measures. Similarly, in Europe, the influx of migrants and refugees from conflict zones and developing countries has prompted varied responses from individual member states, often revealing tensions between national interests and regional humanitarian obligations. The historical evolution of these policies highlights the ongoing struggle to balance federal authority with local governance in the context of immigration, particularly as states grapple with the economic, social, and cultural implications of increased immigration.

The role of public opinion in shaping the discourse on federalism, decentralization, and immigration cannot be overstated.

Historical events, such as economic downturns, terrorist attacks, or shifts in demographic patterns, often profoundly influence public sentiment towards immigration and governance structures. For example, the 2008 financial crisis triggered a surge in anti-immigration sentiment in several European countries, as economic anxieties fueled fears about job competition and the strain on public resources. This, in turn, led to calls for stricter border controls, increased deportations, and a reevaluation of the open border policy within the EU. Similarly, in the United States, changing demographics, economic disparities, and concerns about national security have fueled debates over immigration, with regional governments responding differently based on the prevailing attitudes of their constituents. The rise of anti-immigrant sentiment in certain regions has led to the implementation of restrictive immigration laws and policies, while other areas have maintained more welcoming stances. These historical shifts in public opinion underscore the importance of understanding the socio-political context in which federalism and decentralization operate, particularly regarding immigration policies. Public opinion acts as a crucial feedback loop, influencing political discourse and shaping policy outcomes at both the federal and regional levels.

The ongoing discourse surrounding federalism, decentralization, and immigration is continuously shaped by historical events that influence both political beliefs and policy outcomes. The rise of populist movements in both the U.S. and Europe, often characterized by nativist sentiments and skepticism towards globalization, can be traced back to historical grievances related to perceived loss of sovereignty, cultural erosion, and economic insecurity. As citizens grapple with the perceived negative implications of globalization and increased immigration, these movements often advocate for a return to more centralized control over immigration policies, stricter border enforcement, and the preservation of national identity. This dynamic reflects a broader historical pattern where crises—be they economic, social, or political—serve as catalysts for reexamining the balance between federal governance and regional autonomy. The Brexit vote in the United Kingdom, for example, exemplified this tension. Supporters of Brexit argued for regaining national sovereignty over immigration and trade policies, while opponents warned of the economic and social costs of leaving the EU. Understanding these historical underpinnings is essential for navigating the complexities of current immigration debates and their implications for national identity in both federal and decentralized systems. The rise of populist movements serves as a reminder that the relationship between federalism, decentralization, and immigration is constantly evolving, shaped by historical forces, public opinion, and the ever-changing realities of a globalized world. The future of immigration policy will likely depend on the ability of governments to balance the competing interests of national security, economic opportunity, and social integration, while respecting the diverse identities and values of their citizens.

COMPARATIVE ANALYSIS OF FEDERALISM AND DECENTRALIZATION

STRUCTURAL DIFFERENCES IN GOVERNANCE

The structural differences in governance between federal and decentralized systems are foundational to understanding how policy decisions are made and implemented. Federalism typically involves a division of powers between a central authority and constituent political units, such as states or provinces. This arrangement allows for a balance of power that can cater to diverse regional needs while maintaining a cohesive national policy framework. In contrast, decentralization often signifies the transfer of authority from the central government to local or regional entities, which may operate with significant autonomy. This structural distinction influences how immigration policies are formulated and executed, affecting national identity and cultural integration.

In the context of the United States, federalism plays a critical role in shaping immigration policy. The U.S. Constitution grants states certain powers, allowing them to enact their own immigration regulations in addition to federal laws. This leads to a patchwork of policies that can vary significantly from one state to another. For example, some states may adopt more inclusive practices aimed at integrating immigrants, while others may implement restrictive measures. Such variations not only highlight the complexities of federalism but also provoke debates about national identity, as differing state policies can reflect divergent beliefs about immigration and cultural assimilation.

Conversely, the European Union operates under a more decentralized model, particularly regarding immigration policy. EU member states retain substantial authority to regulate immigration, leading to a wide range of policies that often reflect local cultural beliefs and economic needs. The Schengen Agreement and other EU frameworks provide a degree of coordination among member states, yet the ultimate decision-making power resides with national governments. This can result in significant disparities in how immigration is approached across Europe, raising questions about the effectiveness of collective governance in addressing shared challenges related to migration and integration.

Federalism *and* Immigration *in* the United States

The role of regional governments in both the U.S. and Europe cannot be overstated, as they significantly influence the direction of immigration policies. In federal systems like the U.S., regional governments often serve as laboratories of democracy, experimenting with various approaches to immigration that may later inform national policies. In decentralized contexts, regional governments may prioritize local economic realities or historical contexts, leading to innovative practices that reflect the unique character of their communities. These dynamics underscore the importance of understanding governance structures when analyzing the impact of immigration on national identity and social cohesion.

In the context of the United States, federalism plays a pivotal role in shaping immigration policy. The U.S. Constitution, while granting the federal government broad authority over immigration matters, also reserves certain powers for the states. This inherent tension has resulted in a complex and often contentious landscape where state and federal governments both exert influence on immigration-related issues. States can, for instance, enact their own regulations regarding education, healthcare, and law enforcement as they pertain to immigrants, provided these regulations do not directly contradict federal laws.

This division of power has led to a patchwork of policies that can vary significantly from one state to another. Some states, often those with a history of welcoming immigrants and a strong commitment to diversity, may adopt more inclusive practices aimed at facilitating the integration of newcomers into society. These policies may include offering language assistance programs, providing access to social services regardless of immigration status, and actively promoting cultural understanding. Conversely, other states, often those with concerns about the economic or social impact of immigration, may implement more restrictive measures. These measures might include stricter enforcement of immigration laws, limitations on access to public benefits for undocumented immigrants, and policies designed to deter further immigration.

This variation not only highlights the complexities of federalism but also provokes ongoing debates about national identity. Differing state policies often reflect divergent beliefs about immigration, cultural assimilation, and the role of government in addressing the challenges posed by immigration. For example, the debate over sanctuary cities, municipalities that limit their cooperation with federal immigration authorities, showcases the clash between federal and local priorities and the differing interpretations of national identity. The federal government emphasizes its responsibility to enforce immigration laws uniformly, whereas sanctuary cities prioritize the protection of their residents, regardless of immigration status, arguing that doing so fosters trust and cooperation between law enforcement and immigrant communities.

The structural differences in governance between federalism and decentralization have profound implications for public opinion and political beliefs surrounding immigration. In federal systems, the interplay between state and federal authorities can create tensions that shape public discourse on immigration policy. In decentralized contexts, the influence of regional governments can lead to divergent public sentiments that challenge the notion of a unified national identity. As debates continue across the Atlantic, examining these structural differences will be crucial for addressing the complexities of sovereignty and governance in an increasingly interconnected world.

The sophisticated relationship between governance structures and societal outcomes is particularly evident in the realm of immigration policy. Federalism and decentralization, two distinct approaches to allocating power, significantly influence how nations manage immigration, integrate newcomers, and ultimately, define their national identity. Understanding the structural differences between these systems is fundamental to comprehending the diverse approaches to immigration observed across the United States and the European Union, and the consequent impact on public opinion and political beliefs.

Decentralization *and* Immigration *in the* European Union

Conversely, the European Union operates under a more decentralized model, particularly with regard to immigration policy. While the EU has established certain common frameworks, such as the Schengen Agreement, which allows for free movement within its member states, and the Dublin Regulation, which dictates which member state is responsible for examining an asylum claim, the ultimate authority to regulate immigration largely resides with individual national governments. EU member states retain substantial autonomy to determine their own immigration quotas, set eligibility criteria for visas and residency permits, and enforce immigration laws within their borders.

This decentralized approach has resulted in a wide range of immigration policies across Europe, reflecting the diverse cultural beliefs, economic needs, and political priorities of each member state. For example, Germany, facing labor shortages in certain sectors, has historically adopted a more open immigration policy, particularly for skilled workers. In contrast, countries like Hungary and Poland have taken a more restrictive stance, emphasizing the preservation of national culture and identity.

While the EU strives to coordinate member states' immigration policies through various directives and agreements, the ultimate decision-making power remains with national governments. This can result in significant disparities in how immigration is approached across Europe, raising fundamental questions about the effectiveness of collective governance in addressing shared challenges related to migration and integration. The ongoing debate over the distribution of asylum seekers among EU member states, for instance, underscores the difficulties of achieving a unified approach in a decentralized system.

Some member states, often those located on the periphery of the EU, bear the brunt of asylum applications, while others are reluctant to accept their fair share of responsibility.

The Role *of* Regional Governments

The role of regional governments in both the U.S. and Europe is a cornerstone of governance, particularly when it comes to immigration policies. These subnational entities are not merely administrative extensions of the central government but are active participants in shaping the implementation and impact of immigration policies. Their influence stems from their proximity to local communities, their understanding of regional economic realities, and their capacity to tailor policies to meet specific demographic and social needs. In essence, regional governments serve as crucial intermediaries between national-level mandates and the lived experiences of immigrants and host communities, translating broad policies into targeted actions that directly affect individuals and communities.

In federal systems like the U.S., regional governments, particularly state governments, often serve as "laboratories of democracy," experimenting with various approaches to immigration that may later inform national policies. This experimentation is driven by the inherent flexibility afforded by the federal structure, allowing states to address their unique challenges and opportunities related to immigration. States can pilot innovative programs aimed at integrating immigrants into the workforce, providing educational opportunities, and promoting civic engagement. For example, states with significant agricultural sectors might develop specialized training programs to equip immigrants with the skills necessary for farm work, while states with burgeoning tech industries might focus on attracting and retaining skilled immigrants through targeted recruitment initiatives and streamlined visa processes. The successes and failures of these state-level initiatives can provide valuable insights for federal policymakers seeking to develop more effective and responsive immigration policies, ultimately refining national approaches based on empirical evidence and real-world outcomes.

Furthermore, the laboratory of democracy concept extends beyond programmatic innovation to encompass policy experimentation. States may adopt different approaches to issues such as driver's licenses for undocumented immigrants, tuition policies for immigrant students, and access to social services. These diverse approaches create a natural experiment that allows policymakers and researchers to assess the impact of different policies on various outcomes, such as economic integration, crime rates, and public health. By comparing the experiences of different states, policymakers can gain a better understanding of the potential consequences of different policy choices and make more informed decisions at the national level.

In more decentralized contexts, such as within the European Union, regional governments, often referred to as regions or Länder, possess considerable autonomy in shaping immigration policies within the framework of national and EU laws. This decentralized power allows them to prioritize local economic realities or historical contexts, leading to innovative practices that reflect the unique character of their communities. For example, regions with a long history of immigration, such as certain areas of Germany or France, may have developed sophisticated integration programs that are tailored to the specific needs of their immigrant populations. These programs might include language training, cultural orientation sessions, and vocational training tailored to the local labor market. Other regions may focus on attracting skilled immigrants to address specific labor market demands. For instance, regions with aging populations and shortages of healthcare workers might actively recruit nurses and doctors from abroad, offering incentives such as expedited visa processing and financial assistance for relocation.

These localized approaches underscore the importance of understanding the diverse perspectives and priorities of regional governments when analyzing the impact of immigration on national identity and social cohesion. The needs and concerns of a rural region struggling with population decline are likely to differ significantly from those of a bustling urban center grappling with overcrowding and social inequality. Regional governments are uniquely positioned to understand these nuances and tailor their responses accordingly. By incorporating the perspectives of regional governments into the policymaking process, national governments can develop more effective and equitable immigration policies that address the diverse needs of their populations.

However, the role of regional governments in immigration policy is not without its challenges. The potential for conflicting policies between different regions and between regional and national governments can create confusion and undermine the effectiveness of immigration policies. For example, if one state offers generous social services to immigrants while a neighboring state offers very limited support, it could lead to an influx of immigrants into the state with more generous benefits, potentially straining its resources. Similarly, if a regional government adopts policies that are inconsistent with national immigration laws, it could lead to legal challenges and undermine the rule of law.

Moreover, the capacity of regional governments to effectively implement immigration policies can vary significantly depending on their resources and expertise. Some regions may lack the financial resources or administrative capacity to adequately support immigrant integration programs or enforce immigration laws. This can lead to disparities in outcomes across different regions and undermine the overall effectiveness of national immigration policies.

In conclusion, regional governments play a multifaceted and essential role in shaping immigration policies in both the U.S. and Europe. As "laboratories of democracy" and custodians of local knowledge, they experiment with innovative approaches, tailor policies to regional needs, and provide valuable insights to national policymakers. Recognizing and supporting the crucial role of regional governments is essential for developing effective, responsive, and equitable immigration policies that foster both economic prosperity and social cohesion at all levels of governance. Addressing the challenges related to policy coordination and resource disparities remains crucial to maximizing the benefits of regional engagement in immigration policymaking and ensuring consistent and fair outcomes for immigrants and host communities alike.

Implications *for* Public Opinion *and* Political Beliefs

The structural differences in governance between federalism and decentralization have profound implications for public opinion and political beliefs surrounding immigration. In federal systems, the interplay between state and federal authorities can create tensions that shape public discourse on immigration policy. The contrasting policies and perspectives of state and federal governments can fuel debates about the appropriate balance of power, the role of government in addressing immigration challenges, and the very definition of national identity.

In decentralized contexts, the influence of regional governments can lead to divergent public sentiments that challenge the notion of a unified national identity. When regions adopt significantly different approaches to immigration, it can create divisions within the broader national community, as citizens may identify more strongly with their regional identity than with a shared national identity. This can make it more difficult to achieve consensus on immigration policy and to foster a sense of national unity.

As debates continue across the Atlantic, examining these structural differences will be crucial for addressing the complexities of sovereignty and governance in an increasingly interconnected world. The challenges posed by immigration require a nuanced understanding of the diverse perspectives and priorities of different levels of government, as well as a recognition of the profound impact that governance structures can have on public opinion and political beliefs. By analyzing the experiences of both federal and decentralized systems, policymakers can gain valuable insights into how to design more effective and equitable immigration policies that promote both national unity and the successful integration of newcomers.

Policy-making Processes

Policy-making processes in the context of federalism and decentralization reflect the intricate interplay between governance structures and societal values. In both the United States and the European Union, the formulation of immigration policies showcases how different levels of government interact, negotiate, and sometimes clash over authority. At the federal level, overarching laws and regulations set broad parameters for immigration, while regional governments often adapt these policies to fit local needs and contexts. This duality can create a dynamic policy landscape where the intentions of national directives are reshaped by regional interpretations and practices.

In the U.S., immigration policy has traditionally been a federal prerogative, with laws such as the Immigration and Nationality Act establishing national standards. However, states and municipalities have increasingly sought to exert influence over immigration matters, particularly in response to demographic changes and local economic conditions. This has led to a patchwork of local ordinances and state-level initiatives that both complement and contradict federal policies. The tension between federal authority and state autonomy is a defining feature of the American political landscape, highlighting the complexities of governance in a federal system.

Conversely, the European Union presents a different model of policy-making, where immigration policy is often a collaborative effort among member states. The Schengen Agreement and the Common European Asylum System exemplify attempts to harmonize immigration policies across borders while respecting the sovereignty of individual nations. However, the diverse political climates and cultural attitudes toward immigration within member states can result in significant variations in implementation. This divergence raises questions about the effectiveness of EU-wide policies and the ability of regional governments to address the unique challenges they face in managing immigration.

The impact of immigration policy on national identity is particularly pronounced in both federal and decentralized systems. In the U.S., the narrative of being a nation of immigrants is often juxtaposed with rising sentiments of nationalism, creating friction in public discourse about the role of immigration in shaping American identity. Similarly, in Europe, the influx of migrants has sparked debates about cultural integration and the preservation of national heritage. These discussions not only reflect differing viewpoints on immigration but also illuminate broader questions about how federalism and decentralization influence perceptions of identity and belonging in multicultural societies.

The policy-making processes surrounding immigration in both the U.S. and Europe reveal the significant role of regional governments in shaping discourse and action. By engaging with local populations and addressing specific regional concerns, these governments can effectively influence national policies and contribute to a more nuanced understanding of sovereignty. As immigration continues to be a pressing issue, the examination of federalism versus decentralization in this context offers valuable insights into the future of governance and the evolving nature of national identity across the Atlantic.

Impacts *on* National Identity

The relationship between national identity and the frameworks of governance, particularly federalism and decentralization, is a complex and nuanced topic that merits careful consideration. In both the United States and Europe, these governance models shape how nations perceive themselves and how they integrate diverse populations, especially in the context of immigration. Federal systems tend to promote a more unified national identity, as central governments often craft overarching narratives that emphasize shared values and collective memory. Conversely, decentralized systems can foster regional identities, allowing local cultures and communities to assert their uniqueness within the broader national context. This dynamic creates a multifaceted dialogue about what it means to belong to a nation and how immigration policies influence these identities.

In federal systems like the United States, the central government plays a pivotal role in defining national identity through inclusive immigration policies that either encourage or restrict entry. This can lead to a more homogenized national narrative, where shared ideals of liberty and opportunity are emphasized. The symbolism and rhetoric employed by the federal government, through national holidays, monuments, and educational curricula, further solidify this overarching identity. However, the interplay between federal authority and state-level immigration policies can complicate this narrative, as regional governments may adopt divergent approaches based on local demographics and political climates. For example, states along the U.S.-Mexico border often have unique concerns and policies related to immigration that differ significantly from states in the Northeast. Such variations can result in a patchwork of identities that reflect both the national ethos and regional distinctions, ultimately influencing how immigrants are integrated into society and how they perceive their own identity within the nation. The concept of "American exceptionalism," often promoted at the federal level, can clash with the lived experiences of immigrant communities who face discrimination or economic hardship, leading to a contested and evolving understanding of what it means to be American.

In contrast, decentralized systems, such as those found in many European countries, often allow local governments to tailor immigration policies to better align with regional needs and cultural contexts. This flexibility can lead to a more pluralistic understanding of national identity, where multiple identities coexist and contribute to a shared sense of belonging. Germany, for example, with its strong emphasis on regional autonomy, allows its Länder (states) considerable latitude in implementing integration programs for immigrants. This decentralized approach acknowledges and respects the diverse cultural landscapes within the nation, fostering a sense of belonging that is not necessarily tied to a singular, monolithic national identity. However, the potential for regional fragmentation also raises concerns about national cohesion. As regions assert their identities and priorities regarding immigration, tensions may arise between local and national narratives, complicating the discourse on what it means to be a citizen and how immigrants can fit into these frameworks. The rise of regionalist parties in Europe, often with distinct stances on immigration and national identity, underscores this challenge. Catalonia in Spain, for instance, has often clashed with the central government over issues of cultural preservation and autonomy, reflecting the inherent tensions within decentralized systems.

The impact of immigration policy on national identity is further complicated by the economic implications of federalism and decentralization. In both the U.S. and Europe, regional governments often advocate for policies that reflect local economic conditions and labor market needs. This can lead to immigration policies that favor skilled workers in economically prosperous regions while neglecting the needs of less affluent areas. For example, tech hubs in California may actively seek skilled immigrants in the STEM fields, while rural communities struggling with economic decline may face different pressures and priorities regarding immigration. Such discrepancies not only affect the economic landscape but also shape public perceptions of immigrants, influencing how different communities view national identity and belonging. The perception of immigrants as either economic contributors or a drain on resources can significantly impact social cohesion and the overall narrative of national identity.

Furthermore, the rise of globalization and transnational identities adds another layer of complexity to the relationship between governance, immigration, and national identity. Individuals may simultaneously identify with their nation of origin, their local community, and a global network of shared interests or values. Federal and decentralized systems must grapple with how to accommodate these multiple allegiances and create inclusive frameworks that recognize the fluidity of identity in the 21st century. The internet and social media have facilitated the formation of diasporic communities that transcend national borders, allowing immigrants to maintain strong connections to their homelands while also integrating into their new societies. This phenomenon challenges traditional notions of national identity and citizenship, requiring a more nuanced understanding of belonging.

Moreover, historical legacies of colonialism, slavery, and discrimination continue to shape the discourse on national identity and immigration in both the U.S. and Europe. These legacies have created deep-seated inequalities and prejudices that impact the experiences of immigrants and people of color, often leading to contested narratives of national belonging. The ongoing debates about Confederate monuments in the United States, for instance, reflect the struggle to reconcile competing interpretations of American history and national identity. Similarly, in Europe, the legacies of colonialism continue to influence perceptions of immigrants from former colonies, often perpetuating stereotypes and hindering integration efforts.

The role of education systems in shaping national identity cannot be overlooked. Federal and decentralized governments often use education as a tool to promote specific narratives of national history, culture, and values. The content of textbooks, the celebration of national holidays in schools, and the emphasis on certain historical figures can all contribute to the construction of a particular national identity. However, these educational practices can also be contested, particularly when they exclude or marginalize the experiences of certain groups. Multicultural education initiatives, aimed at promoting a more inclusive and diverse understanding of national identity, have become increasingly common in both the U.S. and Europe, reflecting a growing recognition of the need to address historical injustices and promote social cohesion.

The discourse on sovereignty, federalism, and decentralization is crucial in understanding the evolving nature of national identity in the face of globalization and migration. The interplay between governance structures and immigration policies significantly shapes how identities are constructed, contested, and celebrated. The ability of federal and decentralized systems to adapt to the increasing complexity of identity formation, particularly in the context of immigration, will be crucial for fostering inclusive and cohesive societies. As both the U.S. and Europe navigate these challenges, a commitment to open dialogue, inclusive policies, and a recognition of the value of both national unity and regional diversity will be essential for fostering a more nuanced and equitable understanding of identity in an increasingly interconnected world. This requires not only policy changes but also a fundamental shift in attitudes and perceptions, acknowledging the richness and complexity of human identity in a globalized era.

POLITICAL DISCOURSE ON SOVEREIGNTY

THE CONCEPT OF SOVEREIGNTY IN FEDERAL AND DECENTRALIZED SYSTEMS

The concept of sovereignty in federal and decentralized systems represents a complex interplay of authority, governance, and identity within political frameworks. In federal systems, sovereignty is typically shared between a central government and regional entities, allowing for a division of powers that can accommodate diverse interests and needs. This structure is evident in the United States, where states possess significant legislative authority while still being subject to federal laws. The U.S. Constitution explicitly delineates powers, establishing a system of checks and balances intended to protect local interests while maintaining national unity. This dual sovereignty fosters an environment where regional governments can exercise their powers, particularly in areas such as immigration policy, shaping their unique identities within the broader national narrative.

In contrast, decentralized systems, commonly found within the European Union, manifest sovereignty in a different manner. The European Union operates on principles of shared sovereignty, where member states retain significant autonomy while also ceding certain powers to supranational institutions. This arrangement fosters cooperation and integration among diverse nations, allowing for a more nuanced approach to governance that can address cross-border issues such as immigration. However, the challenge remains in balancing national interests with regional identities, as the EU's decentralized nature can lead to tensions between local governance and overarching EU policies. This tension reflects a broader discourse on how sovereignty is interpreted and enacted across different political landscapes, influencing public opinion and political beliefs.

The impact of immigration policy on national identity is particularly pronounced in both federal and decentralized systems. In the U.S., states have implemented various immigration policies, reflecting their unique demographics and socio-economic conditions. These policies can either align with or diverge from federal regulations, leading to a patchwork of immigration practices that complicate the notion of a singular national identity. Conversely, in the EU, member states grapple with immigration policies that must accommodate both national interests and collective agreements, often resulting in varied approaches that reflect regional cultural beliefs and historical contexts. This divergence illustrates how sovereignty impacts national identity, as each system negotiates the complexities of cultural integration and social cohesion.

Regional governments play a pivotal role in shaping immigration policies within both federal and decentralized frameworks. In the U.S., states like California and Texas have developed distinct immigration strategies that reflect their economic needs and cultural contexts. These regional policies can significantly influence national debates on immigration, underscoring how local governance can assert sovereignty in a manner that impacts broader national discussions. Similarly, in Europe, regional governments often advocate for policies that address local challenges posed by immigration, emphasizing the need for tailored approaches that resonate with their constituents. This dynamic showcases the importance of regional authority in negotiating the terms of sovereignty and identity in the face of global migration trends.

The historical perspectives on federalism and decentralization reveal ongoing trends that shape contemporary political discourse. Both systems are influenced by their historical trajectories, which inform current governance models and the public's perception of sovereignty. In the U.S., the legacy of state rights and federal authority continues to inform debates over immigration, as regional responses evolve in reaction to changing national policies. Meanwhile, the EU's history of integration amidst diverse national identities highlights the challenges of establishing a coherent immigration policy that respects both sovereignty and multiculturalism. As political discourse continues to evolve, the interplay of federalism and decentralization will remain a critical area of study, particularly in understanding how borders and beliefs shape the future of sovereignty in these distinct contexts.

Political Narratives *in the* U.S

Political narratives in the United States are deeply intertwined with the concepts of federalism and decentralization, reflecting a complex interplay between national identity, governance, and immigration policy. Historically, the U.S. has navigated the tension between a strong centralized government and the autonomy of individual states, shaping its political discourse around sovereignty and individual rights. This dichotomy influences how immigration policies are crafted and perceived, with various state governments enacting their own regulations that may either align with or diverge from federal mandates. These narratives not only affect policy outcomes but also resonate with broader societal beliefs about national identity and cultural integration.

In recent years, the political discourse surrounding immigration has become increasingly polarized, with federal and state governments often at odds. On one hand, the federal government may advocate for stricter border controls and enforcement measures, reflecting a narrative that prioritizes national security. Conversely, some states and localities adopt more welcoming approaches to immigrants, emphasizing humanitarian values and the economic contributions of diverse populations. This divergence highlights the complexities of federalism in the U.S., where regional governments play a crucial role in shaping immigration policy based on local economic needs, cultural attitudes, and demographic realities.

The impact of these varying narratives is significant in shaping public opinion and political beliefs regarding immigration. In federal systems, state-level initiatives can serve as laboratories for experimentation, allowing different approaches to be tested in practice. For instance, states with inclusive policies may foster a sense of community and belonging among immigrants, subsequently influencing national debates on immigration reform. This dynamic raises questions about the effectiveness of decentralized governance in addressing immigration challenges, as local policies can either reinforce or challenge prevailing national narratives, further complicating the discourse.

Moreover, the cultural influences on federalism and decentralization play a pivotal role in shaping how immigration policy is perceived and implemented. In regions with a strong historical narrative of immigration as a cornerstone of national identity, local governments may be more inclined to adopt policies that reflect this ethos. In contrast, areas with a more insular perspective may pursue restrictive measures, impacting the broader narrative around immigration in the national context. The interplay of cultural beliefs and political narratives illustrates the importance of understanding regional differences in formulating coherent immigration policies that align with national values.

Examining the political narratives of federalism and decentralization in the U.S. requires a consideration of contemporary trends and historical perspectives. As the dynamics of immigration continue to evolve, the narratives surrounding sovereignty and governance will also shift. The ongoing debates over the role of federal and state governments in immigration policy underscore the need for a nuanced analysis of how these narratives shape and are shaped by public opinion and political beliefs. This ongoing discourse not only informs policy decisions but also reflects the broader challenges of balancing national unity with regional diversity in a multicultural society.

Political Narratives *in* Europe

Political narratives in Europe are shaped by a complex interplay of historical legacies, cultural identities, and contemporary challenges, particularly in the context of federalism and decentralization. The evolution of these narratives reflects the diverse political landscapes across European nations, where varying degrees of central governance coexist with regional autonomy. European countries, such as Germany and Spain, exemplify the federal model, wherein power is shared between national and regional governments. In contrast, nations like France demonstrate a more centralized approach, creating a dynamic discourse around sovereignty and the distribution of power.

The immigration policies across Europe further complicate these narratives, as nations grapple with the socio-political implications of integrating diverse populations. Federal systems often allow regional governments to tailor immigration policies to local needs, which can lead to innovative approaches that reflect the unique cultural contexts of different areas. This localized decision-making can foster a sense of ownership and responsibility, enhancing community cohesion. However, it may also result in disparities in how immigrants are treated, highlighting tensions between regional identities and national narratives of belonging and citizenship.

Cultural influences play a significant role in shaping the political discourse surrounding federalism and decentralization in Europe. Regional identities often inform public opinion and political beliefs, revealing the nuances of how citizens perceive immigration and integration. In regions with strong historical ties and distinct cultural heritages, there may be a push for policies that prioritize local values and traditions. Conversely, in more cosmopolitan areas, there may be a greater emphasis on inclusivity and multiculturalism, reflecting a different understanding of national identity. This divergence in beliefs underscores the complexities inherent in balancing regional autonomy with national unity.

The role of regional governments is critical in shaping immigration policies within the broader European context. These governments not only implement national laws but also have the authority to advocate for localized adaptations that respond to specific demographic challenges. For instance, in regions experiencing significant immigration influxes, local authorities may develop programs aimed at facilitating integration, thereby reinforcing their political narratives. This grassroots approach can lead to innovative solutions that address the needs of both immigrants and long-standing residents, fostering a more harmonious coexistence.

The political narratives surrounding federalism and decentralization in Europe are continually evolving, influenced by historical perspectives, current trends, and public sentiment. As nations navigate the complexities of sovereignty in an increasingly interconnected world, the discourse will likely reflect ongoing debates about the balance of power, the role of regional identities, and the implications of immigration policy on national cohesion. The interplay of these factors will shape the future of European political narratives, as they seek to reconcile local autonomy with broader national interests in a multicultural landscape.

THE ROLE OF REGIONAL GOVERNMENTS

REGIONAL AUTHORITY IN IMMIGRATION POLICY

Regional authority in immigration policy plays a crucial role in shaping the dynamics of federalism and decentralization, particularly in the contexts of the United States and the European Union. In federal systems, such as that of the U.S., states possess significant autonomy to formulate immigration policies tailored to their unique demographic and economic landscapes. This decentralization allows regional governments to respond to local needs and preferences, resulting in a patchwork of policies that can vary widely from one state to another. For instance, states like California and Texas have adopted contrasting approaches to immigration, reflecting their distinct political cultures and economic requirements. This divergence highlights the importance of regional authority in crafting immigration policies that resonate with local populations.

In contrast, the European Union exhibits a different framework for immigration policy, where regional authorities operate within a complex interplay of EU regulations and national laws. Member states retain a degree of sovereignty over immigration while also adhering to overarching EU directives aimed at harmonizing policies across borders. This duality creates a unique landscape where regional governments can influence immigration practices, yet must navigate the constraints imposed by both national governments and EU regulations. The divergent immigration policies among EU nations, such as those seen in Germany versus Hungary, exemplify how regional authorities can advocate for policies that reflect local values and beliefs, even in the face of broader union-wide mandates.

The impact of regional immigration policies is also closely tied to national identity within both federal and decentralized systems. In the U.S., states that embrace more inclusive immigration policies often position themselves as welcoming to immigrants, which can strengthen local economies and foster cultural diversity. Conversely, states that adopt restrictive policies may reinforce a more homogeneous national identity, potentially alienating immigrant populations and undermining economic growth. Similarly, in Europe, nations that adopt progressive immigration policies may enhance their multicultural identities, while those with stringent measures risk reinforcing nationalist sentiments that can fracture social cohesion.

Public opinion plays a significant role in shaping regional authority over immigration policy. In federal systems, regional governments are often more attuned to the sentiments of their constituents, allowing them to implement policies that reflect local beliefs and values. This responsiveness can lead to innovative approaches to immigration, such as community-based integration programs and local labor market initiatives. In the European context, regional authorities may harness public sentiment to advocate for policies that align with local cultural beliefs, influencing national debates on immigration and sovereignty. The interplay between public opinion and regional policy-making highlights the democratic nature of decentralization, where local governments can serve as laboratories for policy experimentation.

Overall, the regional authority in immigration policy underscores the broader themes of sovereignty, federalism, and decentralization in transatlantic discourse. By examining the distinct roles that regional governments play in shaping immigration practices in the U.S. and Europe, one can better understand the complexities of national identity and cultural influences that inform these policies. The comparative analysis reveals not only the challenges posed by differing immigration frameworks but also the potential for regional governments to drive meaningful change in how societies navigate the intricate relationship between borders and beliefs.

CASE STUDIES OF REGIONAL GOVERNMENT ACTIONS

The examination of regional government actions in the context of federalism and decentralization provides valuable insights into how different political structures respond to similar challenges, particularly regarding immigration policy. Case studies from both the United States and European Union illustrate the varying degrees of autonomy and flexibility that regional governments possess in shaping policies that reflect local values and needs. These case studies reveal how regional governments act as important players in the broader discourse on national identity and immigration, often navigating the tensions between central mandates and local priorities.

One prominent example from the United States is California's approach to immigration policy. The state has positioned itself as a sanctuary for undocumented immigrants, enacting laws that limit local law enforcement's cooperation with federal immigration authorities. This action reflects not only California's demographic realities but also the cultural beliefs of its citizens, who largely support more inclusive immigration policies. The state's legislative decisions underscore the role of regional governments in challenging federal directives, illustrating how decentralization can empower local authorities to align immigration policies with the values of their constituents.

In contrast, the experience of Bavaria in Germany highlights how federalism can shape regional responses to immigration in a different context. As one of the wealthiest states in Germany, Bavaria has faced significant immigration influxes, particularly from refugees. The regional government has implemented policies that both facilitate integration and emphasize cultural assimilation, reflecting a balance between welcoming newcomers and preserving regional identity. This case study demonstrates how federal systems can create a dual approach, where regional governments tailor their immigration strategies while adhering to broader national frameworks.

Another instructive case is found in the United Kingdom, where devolved governments in Scotland and Wales have taken distinct stances on immigration. Scotland's government has advocated for a more open immigration policy, arguing that population growth is essential for its economic vitality. In contrast, the Welsh government has focused on integration and community cohesion, emphasizing the need to manage immigration in a way that supports local cultural identities. These divergent approaches reveal how regional governments can influence the national discourse on immigration, reflecting their unique socio-economic contexts and cultural perspectives.

Finally, the case of Spain, particularly Catalonia's efforts to establish its own immigration policies, exemplifies the complexities of regional governance in a decentralized context. Catalonia's push for greater autonomy has extended to immigration, as local authorities seek to implement policies that reflect the region's linguistic and cultural identity. This situation underscores the intersection of immigration policy with broader questions of sovereignty and self-determination, illustrating how regional actions can provoke significant debates within federal systems. These case studies collectively underscore the significance of regional governments in shaping immigration policy, highlighting the dynamic interplay between federalism and decentralization in contemporary political discourse.

Implications *for* National Policy

The implications for national policy surrounding federalism and decentralization in the context of immigration are profound and multifaceted. In both the United States and the European Union, the interaction between national sovereignty and regional autonomy shapes the landscape of immigration policy. As national governments grapple with the challenges posed by migration, the dichotomy between federalism and decentralization becomes increasingly relevant. Policymakers must consider how the distribution of power affects not only the implementation of immigration laws but also the broader questions of national identity and cultural cohesion. The nuances of this relationship call for a deep understanding of the historical, social, and economic factors that influence immigration patterns and policies in different regions. Without this comprehensive perspective, policies may prove ineffective or even counterproductive, exacerbating existing tensions and creating new challenges.

In federal systems, such as that of the United States, the central government typically holds significant authority over immigration policy. This authority is often rooted in constitutional provisions that grant the federal government the power to regulate international trade, control borders, and establish naturalization laws. However, states often possess considerable latitude to influence their own immigration practices, resulting in a patchwork of regulations that can vary dramatically from one region to another. This variation can lead to tensions between state and federal authorities, as seen in debates over sanctuary cities or state-level initiatives that either restrict or promote immigration. For instance, some states have enacted laws requiring local law enforcement to assist federal immigration authorities, while others have implemented policies that limit cooperation. National policy must therefore navigate these complexities, finding a balance that respects regional differences while maintaining a coherent national strategy. This requires careful consideration of the legal boundaries between federal and state authority, as well as a willingness to engage in constructive dialogue with state and local officials to address their concerns and find common ground. Moreover, national policies must be flexible enough to accommodate the diverse needs and priorities of different regions, while still upholding core principles of fairness, equality, and due process.

Conversely, in decentralized systems like those in many European countries, regional governments often play a crucial role in shaping immigration policy. This can lead to innovative approaches tailored to local contexts, but it also raises questions about the consistency and fairness of immigration practices across borders. For example, some regions may prioritize the integration of immigrants into the labor market, while others may focus on providing social services and language training. The European Union's efforts to harmonize immigration policies among member states illustrate the challenges of achieving a unified stance while respecting the autonomy of regional authorities. The Dublin Regulation, which determines the member state responsible for examining an asylum application, has often been criticized for placing undue burden on countries on the EU's external borders. National policymakers must engage in a delicate balancing act, fostering cooperation among regions while ensuring that immigration policies align with broader national objectives. This may involve establishing common standards for immigration enforcement, asylum procedures, and integration programs, while also allowing regions the flexibility to adapt these standards to their specific circumstances. It also requires a commitment to burden-sharing among regions to ensure that no single region is disproportionately affected by immigration pressures.

The impact of immigration policy on national identity is another critical consideration for policymakers. In both federal and decentralized systems, immigration can challenge existing notions of national belonging and cultural homogeneity. As regions adopt differing immigration stances, the resulting diversity can enrich local cultures but may also provoke backlash among populations concerned about preserving traditional identities. The rise of nationalist and anti-immigrant sentiment in many countries reflects these anxieties. National policy must address these concerns by promoting inclusive narratives that recognize the contributions of immigrants while also fostering dialogue about what it means to be a citizen in a multicultural society. This may involve investing in education programs that promote understanding and tolerance, as well as supporting community initiatives that bring together people from different backgrounds. It also requires addressing the economic anxieties that often fuel anti-immigrant sentiment, such as concerns about job competition and wage stagnation. By creating economic opportunities for all members of society, policymakers can help to reduce the perception that immigrants are a threat to the well-being of native-born citizens.

The implications for national policy in the context of federalism and decentralization are far-reaching. The interplay of regional autonomy and national authority shapes not only how immigration laws are crafted and enforced but also the social fabric of societies. Policymakers must remain attuned to the evolving dynamics of immigration in both the U.S. and Europe, drawing on comparative analyses to inform decisions that respect regional identities while promoting a cohesive national vision. This requires a willingness to learn from the successes and failures of other countries, as well as a commitment to evidence-based policymaking. As the discourse on sovereignty continues to evolve, the lessons learned from both systems will be invaluable in crafting effective and equitable immigration policies in the future. Furthermore, the rise of transnational challenges such as climate change and global pandemics necessitates a more collaborative approach to immigration policy, with national governments working together to address the root causes of migration and manage the movement of people across borders in a humane and orderly manner. This requires a shift away from narrow nationalistic perspectives towards a more global and cooperative framework for immigration governance.

CASE STUDIES OF FEDERALISM AND DECENTRALIZATION

Lessons *from* U.S. States

The exploration of federalism and decentralization across U.S. states reveals invaluable lessons regarding governance, particularly in the context of immigration policy. Each state operates under the overarching framework of the U.S. Constitution while possessing the autonomy to enact laws that reflect its unique demographics and cultural influences. This flexibility has allowed states such as California and Texas to develop divergent immigration policies, illustrating how local governance can shape national discourse. Examining these differences provides insight into the interplay between state sovereignty and federal mandates, and highlights the role of regional governments in addressing multicultural challenges.

California, for instance, has positioned itself as a sanctuary state, enacting laws that protect undocumented immigrants and limit cooperation with federal immigration enforcement. This approach has generated significant public support among its diverse population, emphasizing a broader narrative of inclusion and social justice. The state's policies have not only influenced local demographics but have also sparked heated debates at the federal level, challenging the balance of power between state and national authorities. California's experience serves as a compelling case study on how decentralization can empower regional governments to advocate for populations often marginalized in broader national discussions.

Conversely, Texas has adopted a more restrictive stance on immigration, implementing stringent laws aimed at curtailing unauthorized migration. The state's policies reflect a significant portion of its population's beliefs, influenced by cultural attitudes toward immigration and national identity. This divergence from California's approach underscores the complex relationship between regional governance and public opinion. As Texas continues to assert its authority over immigration matters, it raises questions about the efficacy and consequences of such policies on the state's economic landscape and social fabric.

The lessons drawn from these contrasting state experiences extend beyond borders, offering insights applicable to the European context. European nations similarly grapple with the tension between federal structures and regional autonomy, particularly concerning immigration and integration policies. Analyzing the U.S. states provides a framework for understanding how decentralized governance can facilitate tailored responses to immigration, reflecting local values and needs. This comparative analysis encourages European policymakers to consider the benefits and challenges of allowing regional governments greater leeway in shaping immigration policies, given their proximity to diverse communities.

Ultimately, the dynamics of federalism and decentralization in the U.S. serve as a mirror for ongoing debates in Europe regarding sovereignty and national identity. The varying approaches to immigration policy illustrate how regional governments can play a critical role in shaping public discourse and addressing the complexities of multicultural societies. By examining the lessons learned from U.S. states, stakeholders can better navigate the intricate relationship between governance structures and immigration, fostering a more nuanced understanding of sovereignty in the context of an increasingly interconnected world.

Lessons *from* European Regions

The examination of European regions provides valuable insights into the ongoing discourse of federalism versus decentralization, particularly in the context of immigration policy and national identity. Countries such as Germany, Spain, and Belgium exemplify varying degrees of decentralization, each illustrating distinct approaches to governance and the management of cultural diversity. Germany, with its federal structure, allows for significant autonomy at the state level, enabling local governments to tailor immigration policies that reflect regional demographics and economic needs. This flexibility can lead to innovative solutions that address local challenges while contributing to a cohesive national identity.

In contrast, Spain's autonomous communities illustrate the complexities inherent in decentralization. Each region has the authority to implement its immigration policies, which can lead to disparities in how immigrants are integrated into society. For example, Catalonia's proactive stance on integration contrasts sharply with the policies of other regions. This divergence raises questions about the balance between regional autonomy and national coherence. While decentralization encourages local governance, it can also create challenges in fostering a unified national identity, as varying policies may lead to different perceptions of immigration across regions.

Belgium serves as another pertinent case study, revealing the tensions between federalism and the need for cohesive immigration policy. The country's linguistic divide has resulted in distinct regional governments that address immigration in ways reflecting their cultural and linguistic identities. This dynamic showcases how cultural beliefs can influence immigration policies, often complicating the broader national narrative. The interplay between regional and federal authorities in

Belgium highlights the importance of dialogue and cooperation in managing immigration effectively while respecting regional identities.

Furthermore, the economic implications of federalism and decentralization in the context of immigration are significant. Regions with more decentralized governance often have tailored immigration policies that align with their economic needs, potentially attracting diverse talent and labor. For instance, regions in Northern Italy have developed specific strategies to draw in skilled workers, thereby enhancing their economic competitiveness. This localized approach to immigration can serve as a model for other regions grappling with demographic shifts and labor market demands, emphasizing the need for policies that are responsive to regional economic contexts.

Ultimately, the lessons from European regions underscore the importance of understanding the interplay between governance structures and immigration policy. By analyzing how different regions navigate the challenges of immigration through federalism and decentralization, policymakers can glean valuable insights applicable to both the European and American contexts. This comparative analysis not only enriches the discourse on national identity and immigration but also highlights the need for adaptable and inclusive governance frameworks that can respond to the complexities of a multicultural society.

Comparative Outcomes *and* Best Practices

In examining the comparative outcomes of federalism and decentralization, it becomes crucial to explore how these governance structures influence and shape immigration policies in both the United States and Europe. The distinct approaches adopted by federal and decentralized systems provide valuable insights into the effectiveness of policy implementation and the resultant societal impacts. Federal systems often enable a unified national policy framework, which, while providing consistency, can sometimes overlook regional variations and local needs. In contrast, decentralized systems allow for localized governance, facilitating tailored immigration policies that reflect the unique demographic and cultural contexts of different regions.

The best practices in immigration policy within federal systems often hinge on balancing state and national interests. For instance, the U.S. federal structure permits states to implement their own immigration laws, leading to a patchwork of policies that can cause confusion and disparity. However, successful states leverage this autonomy to innovate and respond to specific regional challenges, such as labor shortages or demographic shifts. The interplay between state and national policies demonstrates the importance of dialogue and collaboration between different levels of government in achieving cohesive immigration strategies that respect both local autonomy and national objectives.

On the other hand, in decentralized systems like those found in parts of Europe, the role of regional governments is paramount in shaping immigration policies. These governments often have the flexibility to address the needs of their populations directly, leading to more responsive and culturally sensitive policy-making. For example, regions with significant immigrant populations may develop programs that promote integration and social cohesion, reflecting the values and beliefs of their communities. By examining case studies from various European regions, it becomes evident that decentralized governance can foster innovative solutions to immigration challenges, ultimately enhancing national identity while respecting regional diversity.

Cultural influences play a pivotal role in the immigration discourse across both federal and decentralized systems. In federal structures, national narratives about identity can conflict with local sentiments, creating tensions that complicate the implementation of immigration policies. In decentralized contexts, regional identities can significantly shape immigration approaches, leading to varied public opinions and political beliefs. Understanding these cultural dimensions is essential for policymakers aiming to navigate the complexities of immigration in multicultural societies, as they must consider how deeply held beliefs influence both public perception and policy effectiveness.

The comparative analysis of federalism and decentralization reveals a spectrum of outcomes influenced by governance structures, cultural contexts, and political discourses surrounding sovereignty. Best practices emerge from recognizing that no one-size-fits-all solution exists; rather, successful immigration policies must adapt to the unique needs and beliefs of each region. By learning from both American and European experiences, policymakers can develop frameworks that not only facilitate effective immigration management but also promote national cohesion and respect for regional diversity in an increasingly interconnected world.

PUBLIC OPINION AND POLITICAL BELIEFS

SURVEYING PUBLIC ATTITUDES TOWARD FEDERALISM AND DECENTRALIZATION

The examination of public attitudes toward federalism and decentralization reveals significant insights into how these political structures are perceived across the Atlantic. In both the United States and Europe, the discourse surrounding federalism often intertwines with issues of national identity, particularly as it relates to immigration policy. Understanding public sentiment in this context is crucial for policymakers who seek to navigate the complex interplay between regional autonomy and national cohesion. Survey data indicates that attitudes toward federalism and decentralization can vary widely depending on factors such as regional identity, historical context, and current socio-political circumstances.

In the United States, public opinion on federalism has been shaped by a long-standing tradition of states' rights and local governance. Many Americans view decentralization as a means to enhance democratic participation and tailor policies to local needs. This sentiment is particularly pronounced in regions that have experienced significant demographic changes due to immigration. As local governments grapple with the challenges and opportunities posed by new populations, public attitudes often reflect a desire for flexibility in immigration policy that aligns with regional values and priorities. In contrast, there exists a segment of the population that perceives federalism as a potential threat to national unity, particularly in times of economic uncertainty or social unrest.

European attitudes toward federalism and decentralization are equally complex, influenced by the continent's diverse cultural, linguistic, and historical diversity. Public sentiment towards decentralization often varies among EU member states, with countries like Germany embracing a federal structure that empowers regional governments, while others, such as France, maintain a more centralized approach. Surveys indicate that in regions with high levels of immigration, there is a growing demand for decentralized governance that allows for tailored responses to the unique challenges posed by multicultural societies. This is particularly relevant in the context of the European Union's immigration policies, which have often been criticized for their one-size-fits-all approach.

The impact of immigration policy on national identity plays a pivotal role in shaping public attitudes toward federalism and decentralization. In both the U.S. and Europe, debates about immigration are often intertwined with discussions about what it means to be part of a nation. For some, decentralization is viewed as a means to preserve local cultures and identities in the face of globalization and immigration. Conversely, others argue that a strong federal response is necessary to maintain a cohesive national identity. These divergent views reflect deeper beliefs about sovereignty, belonging, and the role of government in the lives of individuals.

The intersection of public opinion, immigration policy, and the structures of governance presents a compelling area for further research and analysis. As both the U.S. and Europe continue to navigate the challenges of globalization and demographic change, understanding how public attitudes toward federalism and decentralization evolve will be crucial. Policymakers must grapple with the implications of these attitudes for immigration policy, national identity, and the broader discourse on sovereignty. By fostering a more nuanced understanding of public sentiment, political leaders can better address the aspirations and concerns of their constituents within the framework of federalism and decentralization.

Political Beliefs *and* Immigration Debates

Political beliefs play a critical role in shaping the immigration debates that resonate across both the American and European contexts. As societies engage with the complexities of immigration, political perspectives often reflect deeper ideological divides pertaining to federalism and decentralization. In the United States, immigration policy is frequently framed within a federalist context, where the balance of power between state and federal authorities influences how laws are enacted and enforced. Conversely, in the European Union, immigration discourse is complicated by the presence of multiple sovereign states, each with its own set of values and approaches to immigration, leading to varying degrees of decentralization in policy implementation.

The impact of immigration policy on national identity is particularly pronounced in federal versus decentralized systems. In federal nations, such as the U.S., immigration policies can directly affect perceptions of national identity, often leading to a more homogenized view that prioritizes national sovereignty. The central government's ability to shape broad immigration policies can create a unified national identity, albeit at the potential expense of regional diversity. In contrast, decentralized systems like those found in many EU countries allow for regional governments to enact tailored immigration policies that reflect local cultural values and needs, fostering a more pluralistic identity that can both enrich and challenge the notion of a cohesive national identity.

Cultural influences significantly affect political beliefs regarding immigration and the approaches taken by federal and decentralized systems. In the U.S., political polarization is evident, with immigration often becoming a contentious issue that divides parties and communities. The beliefs surrounding immigration are shaped by historical narratives, economic concerns, and social dynamics that vary across states. Meanwhile, in Europe, cultural heritage and historical migration patterns inform regional responses to immigration, leading to a patchwork of policies that reflect both regional identities and collective European values. This cultural dimension complicates the discourse surrounding sovereignty, as nations grapple with their historical responsibilities and the contemporary challenges of immigration.

The role of regional governments in shaping immigration policies is crucial in both contexts. In the U.S., states may push back against federal regulations, advocating for more localized control over immigration enforcement and integration efforts. This can lead to innovative approaches that address specific community needs but may also create tensions between state and federal authorities. In Europe, regional governments often have the autonomy to set immigration policies that align with local labor market demands and cultural contexts, emphasizing the importance of regional governance in managing the demographic changes brought about by immigration. Such dynamics highlight the importance of understanding the interplay between political beliefs, regional governance, and immigration policy.

Finally, public opinion and political beliefs are closely intertwined with the debates on immigration within both federal and decentralized systems. In the U.S., shifts in public sentiment can swiftly influence immigration policy, often reflecting broader political trends and party ideologies. In Europe, public opinion is similarly pivotal, leading to diverse responses that can either promote inclusivity or foster exclusionary practices. Political beliefs surrounding immigration are not static; they evolve in response to economic conditions, security concerns, and cultural shifts, reflecting the complexities of managing immigration in a globalized world. As both regions navigate these challenges, the ongoing discourse on sovereignty, federalism, and decentralization will continue to shape the future of immigration policy and its broader implications for national identity.

The Role *of* Media *in* Shaping Discourse

The media wields significant influence in shaping discourse around complex issues such as federalism and decentralization, particularly within the volatile contexts of immigration policy and national identity. Both the United States and the European Union serve as prime examples of regions where media narratives not only mirror public opinion but also actively mold it, frequently framing immigration as a central issue in discussions of sovereignty, cultural integration, and economic stability. Through a diverse array of platforms—spanning traditional news outlets, burgeoning social media networks, and various public forums—the media disseminates information, selectively highlights specific narratives, and often sets the agenda that dominates political and societal conversations. This active shaping of discourse can either reinforce or fundamentally challenge existing beliefs about the optimal balance between federal and local power, significantly impacting how citizens perceive the role and effectiveness of government at different levels.

In the American context, the media's portrayal of immigration can have a profound effect on public support for federal versus state-level policies. Local news stories often emphasize the actions and initiatives of regional governments in managing immigration, showcasing the distinct challenges and strategies employed in different locales. This focused attention on regional responses can foster a perception that decentralization is not only more responsive but also more effective in addressing the nuanced concerns and unique demographics of specific communities. Conversely, national media outlets may opt to frame immigration as a predominantly federal issue, focusing on broader trends, national-level policies, and the overarching implications for the country as a whole. This macro-level perspective can inadvertently dilute the perceived importance of regional perspectives, contributing to a sense that immigration requires a unified, top-down approach. This dynamic interplay creates a complex media environment where representations can either empower local authorities, by highlighting their successes and responsiveness, or reinforce federal dominance, by emphasizing the need for national cohesion and standardized enforcement. This, in turn, profoundly shapes the public's understanding of sovereignty in immigration matters, influencing their beliefs about which level of government is best equipped to handle the challenges and opportunities presented by immigration.

Similarly, in Europe, the media plays a pivotal role in shaping the discourse on federalism versus decentralization through its coverage of immigration policies across member states. The EU's often debated and criticized approach to immigration is frequently scrutinized through the lens of national identity, with media narratives often highlighting the perceived cultural, economic, and social implications of immigration on national sovereignty. Regional governments within Europe, such as those in Spain, Italy, or Germany, often find themselves taking center stage in media stories, showcasing their unique approaches to immigration management amidst the overarching framework of EU regulations and directives. These regional narratives can emphasize the tensions between national interests and EU mandates, leading to a heightened awareness of the critical role that regional governance plays in shaping both policy outcomes and public sentiment, potentially challenging the notion of a singular, harmonized federal approach to immigration. The media's focus on regional variations in immigration policy can also expose the diverse challenges and opportunities faced by different regions, further complicating the debate about the appropriate level of governance.

The impact of media on public opinion cannot be overstated, particularly in multicultural societies where beliefs and values about immigration are often deeply ingrained and vary widely across different demographic groups. Through selective reporting, strategic framing of issues, and the amplification of certain voices over others, the media can either actively support a narrative of inclusion, diversity, and the benefits of immigration, or, conversely, fuel fears of cultural dilution, economic strain, and potential security risks. This power to shape perceptions becomes particularly significant in federal and decentralized systems, such as the US and the EU, where regional governments may advocate for markedly different immigration policies based on their specific needs, priorities, and historical contexts. The media's portrayal of these diverse policies directly influences how citizens perceive their own identity in relation to national narratives, impacting their support for either federal oversight and standardization or local autonomy and responsiveness in immigration matters. For example, a media narrative that highlights the economic contributions of immigrants in a particular region may strengthen support for decentralized immigration policies that cater to the specific labor needs of that region, whereas a narrative that focuses on the potential strain on social services may bolster support for more centralized, restrictive policies.

Furthermore, social media has emerged as a particularly potent force in shaping discourse on immigration and federalism. The rapid dissemination of information, often unfiltered and unverified, can quickly amplify both positive and negative narratives about immigration, impacting public opinion in real time. Social media platforms also allow for the formation of echo chambers, where individuals are primarily exposed to information that confirms their existing beliefs, further polarizing the debate on immigration and the appropriate role of federal versus local governments. The proliferation of fake news and disinformation on social media also poses a significant challenge to informed public discourse, as it can easily spread misinformation and sow distrust in both government institutions and traditional media outlets.

In conclusion, the media serves as a powerful actor in shaping discourse surrounding federalism and decentralization, particularly in the context of immigration policy. By influencing public perceptions, framing critical issues, and amplifying certain voices over others, the media plays a vital role in the ongoing debate about sovereignty in both the United States and Europe. This role is further amplified by the rise of social media, which allows for the rapid dissemination of information and the formation of echo chambers. Understanding the media's multifaceted impact, including both its potential to inform and its capacity to distort, is essential for comprehending the complexities of political discourse in these regions, as it both reflects and shapes the evolving dynamics of federalism, decentralization, and national identity in the face of pressing immigration challenges. A critical and discerning approach to media consumption is crucial for citizens to form informed opinions and participate effectively in the democratic process.

Future Directions
Summary *of* Key Findings

The examination of key findings in the discourse surrounding federalism and decentralization reveals significant distinctions and overlaps between the United States and European Union. One major finding is that federal systems tend to create a more unified national identity, while decentralized systems often accommodate diverse regional identities. This divergence impacts how immigration policies are formed and implemented, as federal systems generally benefit from more centralized decision-making processes that can streamline immigration regulations. Conversely, decentralized systems may lead to a patchwork of immigration policies that reflect the cultural and political preferences of individual regions, potentially fostering both innovation and inconsistency.

Another crucial element identified in this analysis is the role of regional governments in shaping immigration policy. In federal systems like the U.S., states hold considerable power, but executive authority often balances regional interests with national priorities. In contrast, European nations exhibit varying levels of decentralization, with some regions having significant autonomy over immigration matters. This leads to the conclusion that regional governments are not merely passive players; rather, they actively influence the immigration discourse, reflecting local beliefs and cultural contexts. As a result, immigration policies in both systems are shaped by the interplay between regional autonomy and national frameworks.

Cultural influences also emerge as a significant factor in the federalism versus decentralization debate. The findings suggest that public opinion and political beliefs about immigration are deeply entrenched in historical narratives and societal values. In the U.S., narratives of the "melting pot" continue to inform federal immigration policies, while in Europe, the emphasis on national identity often complicates the integration of immigrants. These cultural dimensions play a pivotal role in determining how various regions approach immigration, revealing that social and cultural contexts are as important as legal frameworks in shaping policy outcomes.

Furthermore, the economic implications of federalism and decentralization on immigration cannot be overlooked. The analysis indicates that regions with decentralized systems tend to adopt immigration policies that reflect local economic needs, potentially leading to more responsive labor markets. However, the disparity in resources among regions can also create challenges, as wealthier areas may attract more immigrants, exacerbating regional inequalities. In contrast, federal systems can impose uniform policies that aim to balance economic growth with social integration, yet may struggle to address local labor demands effectively.

Finally, the political discourse surrounding sovereignty in the context of federalism and decentralization reveals a complex landscape. The findings indicate that debates over immigration often invoke deep-seated beliefs about national sovereignty and identity, influencing both public opinion and policy frameworks. This discourse is particularly relevant in transatlantic relations, where differing perspectives on governance and autonomy shape how immigration is viewed. As such, understanding the nuances of federalism and decentralization is essential for policymakers and scholars alike, as they navigate the challenges posed by immigration in increasingly multicultural societies.

The Future *of* Federalism *and* Decentralization

The future of federalism and decentralization is increasingly shaped by the evolving dynamics of globalization, migration, and cultural identity. As nation-states grapple with the complexities of immigration and the pressures of diverse populations, the tension between centralized governance and local autonomy becomes more pronounced. In the context of the U.S. and the EU, federalism often embodies a balancing act between national interests and regional identities, while decentralization promotes localized decision-making that reflects the unique characteristics of diverse communities. The trajectory of these governance models will significantly influence how societies address pressing issues, particularly immigration, which continues to challenge traditional notions of sovereignty and national identity.

In the United States, federalism has historically provided a framework for states to tailor immigration policies to their specific needs, leading to a patchwork of regulations that can either facilitate or hinder integration. As regional governments exert more influence over immigration policy, the implications for national identity become complex. The divergence in state laws regarding immigration reflects varying cultural beliefs and political ideologies, suggesting that the future of federalism will hinge on the ability of states to navigate these differences while contributing to a cohesive national identity. This trend may foster a more nuanced understanding of belonging, as regional identities gain prominence alongside national narratives.

Conversely, the European Union's approach to decentralization raises questions about the effectiveness of collective immigration policies in the face of diverse cultural landscapes. The EU's framework encourages member states to retain significant control over their immigration systems, often leading to disparities in how migrants are treated across borders. As public opinion shifts and the political climate becomes more polarized, the future of decentralization in Europe may rest on the ability of regional governments to engage in collaborative governance while respecting the sovereignty of individual states. This relationship between regional autonomy and collective action will be crucial in addressing the challenges posed by migration and integration.

Additionally, the intersection of immigration policy and federalism in multicultural societies will play a pivotal role in shaping public discourse. As communities become more diverse, the expectations of local governments to manage immigration effectively will increase. The effectiveness of federalism and decentralization will depend on how well regional authorities can respond to the needs of their constituents while aligning with broader national objectives. This requires a delicate balance, especially as public opinion regarding immigration becomes more polarized, potentially leading to conflicts between regional aspirations and national policies.

The future of federalism and decentralization will be determined by the interplay of political beliefs, cultural influences, and economic considerations. As both the U.S. and EU navigate the complexities of immigration policy, the lessons learned from comparative analyses of their federal and decentralized systems will be invaluable. The ongoing discourse surrounding sovereignty, borders, and beliefs will shape how societies reconcile their national identities with the realities of an interconnected world. As we look ahead, it is clear that the evolution of these governance models will significantly impact the resilience and adaptability of democratic institutions in the face of changing societal dynamics.

Recommendations *for* Policy *and* Research

To navigate the complexities of federalism versus decentralization, policymakers should consider a comprehensive approach that integrates the unique historical and cultural contexts of both the United States and Europe. This necessitates a dialogue between federal and regional authorities, promoting collaboration over competition. Engaging local governments in the development of immigration policies can enhance both effectiveness and public acceptance, as regional governments often possess a better understanding of their communities' needs. Therefore, encouraging frameworks that facilitate intergovernmental cooperation can lead to more nuanced and responsive immigration policies that reflect local values while adhering to national standards.

Research initiatives must focus on comparative studies that illuminate the varying impacts of federalism and decentralization on immigration policy. By examining case studies from different regions, scholars can identify best practices and potential pitfalls associated with each governance style. Such analysis will not only deepen our understanding of how immigration policies shape national identity but also provide insights into how cultural influences play a pivotal role in shaping public attitudes toward immigration. This research should be interdisciplinary, drawing from political science, sociology, and economics, to create a holistic view of the implications of immigration within federal and decentralized systems.

In exploring the intersection of immigration policy and federalism, it is crucial to consider the economic implications of these governance structures. Policymakers should prioritize research that assesses the economic outcomes of varying immigration policies across federal and decentralized frameworks. This includes analyzing how different governance models affect labor markets, economic growth, and social cohesion. By understanding these dynamics, policymakers can design immigration strategies that not only align with national identity but also contribute positively to economic stability and growth in both the U.S. and EU contexts.

Moreover, public opinion plays a significant role in shaping immigration debates within federal and decentralized systems. To craft effective policies, it is essential to conduct surveys and studies that capture the sentiments of diverse populations regarding immigration. This data can inform policymakers about the prevailing beliefs and concerns within communities, allowing for the development of policies that resonate with public sentiment. Engaging citizens in discussions about immigration can foster a sense of ownership and responsibility, ultimately leading to more sustainable and accepted immigration policies.

The role of regional governments in shaping immigration policies cannot be overstated. Policymakers should support initiatives that empower local authorities to create tailored immigration strategies that reflect their unique demographics and cultural contexts. This decentralized approach not only enhances responsiveness but also encourages innovation in addressing immigration challenges. By fostering a system where regional governments can experiment with different policies, we can obtain valuable insights that inform broader national strategies, ensuring that immigration policies are both effective and aligned with the values of diverse communities across the Atlantic.

BRIDGING THE ATLANTIC POLITICAL LESSONS FROM EUROPE AND THE U.S

INTRODUCTION TO TRANSATLANTIC POLITICAL DYNAMICS

Overview of European *and* US Political Landscapes

The political landscapes of Europe and the United States present a complex interplay of historical context, cultural values, and institutional frameworks that shape their governance and public policy. At the core of this comparison lies the welfare state model, which varies significantly between the two regions. European countries tend to embrace a more comprehensive welfare system that prioritizes social safety nets and universal healthcare, while the US model is characterized by a more market-oriented approach with limited government involvement in providing social services. This divergence in welfare policies informs broader discussions about economic equity, social justice, and the role of government in citizens' lives, highlighting the advantages and challenges inherent in each system.

Electoral systems also play a crucial role in shaping political representation on both sides of the Atlantic. In Europe, many countries utilize proportional representation, allowing for a wider array of political parties to gain seats in legislative bodies. This system encourages coalition governments and often results in more diverse viewpoints being represented in policy discussions. Conversely, the US employs a first-past-the-post electoral system, which often leads to a two-party dominance, limiting the political spectrum and stifling third-party emergence. The implications of these differing electoral frameworks extend beyond representation; they influence voter engagement, political polarization, and the overall health of democratic practices.

Political parties are pivotal in both European and US contexts, acting as conduits for public policy formation and representation of various interest groups. In Europe, political parties often align closely with ideological movements, resulting in well-defined party platforms that reflect the nuances of voters' preferences. This contrasts with the US, where parties may exhibit broader ideologies that can sometimes obscure distinct policy positions. The role of parties in shaping public discourse, mobilizing voters, and influencing legislation is significant in both regions, yet the effectiveness and accountability of these parties vary greatly due to their structural differences and the political culture that surrounds them.

The historical context of each region has left a lasting impact on contemporary political ideologies. In Europe, the aftermath of World War II and the subsequent Cold War shaped a collective commitment to social democracy and human rights, fostering an environment that values community welfare. In contrast, the US political ideology has been heavily influenced by individualism and capitalism, promoting a belief in limited government and personal responsibility. These underlying principles continue to influence contemporary debates on issues such as immigration, environmental policy, and gender representation, revealing the deep-seated values that drive political decisions in each region.

The rise of populism is another critical element in the transatlantic political dialogue, reflecting broader discontent with traditional political institutions. Both Europe and the US have witnessed the emergence of populist movements that challenge established parties, often leveraging economic anxiety and cultural grievances. These movements highlight the growing divide in political ideologies and the need for a nuanced understanding of public sentiment. As the political landscapes evolve, examining the lessons learned from each region can provide valuable insights for bridging divides and fostering collaborative approaches to global challenges, including environmental policies and governance strategies that address the needs of diverse populations.

Historical Context *of* Transatlantic Relations

The historical context of transatlantic relations is essential for understanding the intricacies of contemporary political dynamics between Europe and the United States. The roots of these relations can be traced back to the colonial period when European powers, particularly Britain, established settlements in the New World. This initial connection laid the groundwork for a complex interplay of cultural, political, and economic exchanges that would evolve over centuries. The American Revolution marked a pivotal moment, as it not only severed colonial ties but also inspired revolutionary movements in Europe, highlighting a shared value in democratic ideals and self-governance. However, this shared aspiration was tempered by diverging interpretations of liberty and governance, setting the stage for future transatlantic debates. The nascent United States grappled with forming a durable republic, while Europe continued to navigate monarchical legacies and emerging nationalist sentiments.

The 19th and early 20th centuries witnessed significant developments that shaped transatlantic relations, including industrialization, immigration, and the rise of national identities. The waves of European immigrants to the United States contributed to the country's demographic and cultural diversity, while also fostering connections with their countries of origin. These immigrants brought with them not only their traditions and skills but also their political ideologies and experiences, enriching the American political landscape and influencing labor movements, social reforms, and foreign policy perspectives. Political ideologies began to take shape in response to these changes, with the emergence of socialism, liberalism, and various nationalist movements in Europe, contrasted by the American experience of frontier individualism and capitalist expansion. These differing political paradigms influenced the evolution of political parties and their platforms on both sides of the Atlantic. For instance, the rise of labor parties in Europe, advocating for workers' rights and social welfare, contrasted with the more laissez-faire approach to economic regulation prevalent in the United States, albeit with growing calls for reform. This divergence was further exacerbated by the American Civil War, which exposed deep divisions within the young nation and had significant ramifications for its international standing and relationship with European powers, some of whom saw economic opportunities in supporting the Confederacy.

The aftermath of World War II marked another critical juncture in transatlantic relations, as the United States and Western European nations sought to rebuild and stabilize their economies. The devastation wrought by the war forced a reassessment of global power dynamics and the need for international cooperation. Institutions such as the Marshall Plan and NATO symbolized a commitment to collective security and economic cooperation. The Marshall Plan, in particular, was instrumental in rebuilding Western Europe's infrastructure and economy, fostering a sense of shared destiny and solidifying the alliance against the Soviet Union. However, the Cold War also introduced new tensions and complexities. While united against a common enemy, disagreements arose over strategic approaches, burden-sharing within NATO, and the degree of intervention in global conflicts. Moreover, the establishment of welfare state models in various European countries offered a contrasting approach to social policy compared to the United States. This divergence in welfare state frameworks would later become a significant point of comparison, influencing public policy debates and political discourse on both sides. The European emphasis on universal healthcare, generous social safety nets, and robust labor protections stood in stark contrast to the more market-oriented and individualistic approach in the United States, fostering ongoing debates about the role of government in society.

The late 20th century and early 21st century brought new challenges and transformations, including the collapse of the Soviet Union, globalization, the rise of populism, and political polarization. The end of the Cold War initially seemed to usher in an era of unprecedented cooperation and multilateralism. However, new challenges soon emerged, including the rise of terrorism, economic crises, and the increasing interconnectedness of global markets. Globalization, while fostering economic growth and cultural exchange, also led to anxieties about job displacement, income inequality, and the erosion of national sovereignty. Populist movements gained traction in both Europe and the United States, often fueled by economic anxieties and disillusionment with traditional political parties. These movements have reshaped electoral systems and political representation, raising questions about governance and the role of political parties in addressing public concerns. The 2008 financial crisis exposed vulnerabilities in the global financial system and led to differing policy responses on both sides of the Atlantic, further highlighting the diverging economic philosophies. The contrasting approaches to immigration and environmental policy further illustrate how historical context continues to influence contemporary political ideologies and debates across the Atlantic. The European Union's more integrated approach to climate change mitigation, for example, contrasts with the more cautious and often skeptical stance towards international agreements in certain segments of the American political spectrum. Similarly, debates surrounding immigration policy reflect differing histories of immigration, integration, and national identity formation.

Furthermore, the rise of supranational organizations like the European Union has significantly altered the transatlantic relationship. While initially viewed as a positive development, promoting peace and economic integration, the EU has also become a source of tension due to perceived infringements on national sovereignty and differing views on trade, security, and foreign policy. The UK's decision to leave the EU, for instance, has had profound implications for transatlantic relations, raising questions about the future of European integration and the alignment of interests between the United States and Europe. Furthermore, issues such as data privacy, digital taxation, and the regulation of technology companies have emerged as new areas of contention, reflecting differing regulatory philosophies and economic priorities. The increasing emphasis on national security and economic protectionism in both Europe and the United States has further complicated the transatlantic relationship, leading to trade disputes and disagreements over strategic alliances.

In summary, the historical context of transatlantic relations reveals the complex interplay of cultural, political, and economic factors that have shaped the political landscape on both sides. Understanding these historical developments is crucial for examining how contemporary issues, such as gender representation, political polarization, the influence of supranational organizations, and the challenges of climate change and cybersecurity, are framed within a transatlantic perspective. By analyzing these dynamics, we can identify lessons that inform future collaboration and dialogue between Europe and the United States in addressing shared challenges and opportunities. A nuanced understanding of the historical underpinnings of transatlantic relations is essential for navigating the complexities of the 21st century and ensuring a future of continued cooperation and mutual understanding, even amidst inevitable disagreements and diverging priorities. The ability to appreciate the different historical trajectories, political cultures, and societal values on both sides of the Atlantic will be crucial for fostering a strong and resilient transatlantic partnership in a rapidly changing world.

ANALYZING POLITICAL PARTIES ACROSS THE ATLANTIC

THE ROLE OF POLITICAL PARTIES IN EUROPE

The role of political parties in Europe is multifaceted and significantly shapes the continent's political landscape. Unlike the United States, where a dominant two-party system prevails, many European countries operate within multiparty systems. This diversity enables a broader representation of viewpoints, facilitating coalitions that can lead to more comprehensive public policies. Political parties in Europe often align themselves with specific ideological frameworks, such as social democracy, liberalism, or conservatism, allowing for a rich variety of political discourse that reflects the varied interests of the populace.

European political parties also play a critical role in shaping public policy by acting as intermediaries between citizens and the government. They articulate the interests and concerns of their constituents, translating them into legislative agendas. This process is often more transparent and participatory than in the U.S., where political parties can be seen as more hierarchical and centralized. In Europe, grassroots movements within parties can influence policy direction, leading to a dynamic interplay between party leadership and membership that encourages responsiveness to public sentiment.

Additionally, the historical context of Europe has greatly influenced contemporary political ideologies and party dynamics. The legacy of World War II, the Cold War, and the subsequent European integration has fostered a unique political environment characterized by a commitment to multilateralism and social welfare. Political parties in Europe often prioritize collective values and social justice, reflecting a historical understanding of the need for solidarity in the face of past divisions. This contrasts with the U.S. political landscape, where individualism and market-oriented policies are more prevalent.

Electoral systems in Europe also contribute to the effectiveness of political parties in representing diverse interests. Proportional representation, common in many European nations, encourages smaller parties to gain seats in parliament, ensuring that minority views are included in the political dialogue. This stands in stark contrast to the U.S.'s winner-takes-all approach, which can marginalize smaller parties and limit political diversity. The implications of these differing electoral systems are profound, as they influence not only party formation but also voter engagement and satisfaction with the political process.

Lastly, the rise of populism in both Europe and the U.S. highlights the challenges faced by traditional political parties. In Europe, populist movements have emerged in response to economic crises, immigration, and dissatisfaction with the political establishment. These movements often capitalize on public discontent and challenge the status quo, prompting established parties to reassess their strategies and policies. The transatlantic perspective on these developments underscores the necessity for political parties to adapt and evolve in response to changing voter sentiments, ensuring they remain relevant in an increasingly polarized political environment.

The Role *of* Political Parties *in the* U.S

Political parties in the United States serve as essential vehicles for political organization, representation, and policy-making. Unlike many European countries, where multi-party systems often dominate, the U.S. operates primarily under a two-party system, consisting of the Democratic and Republican parties. This structure significantly shapes the political landscape, influencing electoral outcomes and governance. Political parties in the U.S. not only mobilize voters but also provide a framework for political discourse, shaping the ideological contours of public policy. The mechanisms of party operation and their interaction with the electoral system highlight the unique dynamics at play in American politics.

The historical context of political parties in the U.S. reveals a trajectory marked by evolution and adaptation. Originating from the early factions in the late 18th century, American political parties have transformed in response to changing societal needs and pressures. The emergence of key issues, such as civil rights, economic policy, and healthcare, has driven the parties to redefine their platforms and alignments. This process of realignment has often reflected the broader societal shifts, paralleling changes in demographics, economic conditions, and cultural attitudes. Understanding this historical evolution is crucial for grasping how contemporary political ideologies are formed and contested within the U.S. political framework.

In contrast to European political parties, which frequently engage with a wider spectrum of ideological positions due to their multi-party systems, U.S. parties tend to be more polarized. This polarization has profound implications for governance and policy-making, often resulting in gridlock and a lack of bipartisan cooperation. The rigid party lines can stifle compromise, making it challenging to address pressing issues such as climate change, healthcare reform, and immigration. This phenomenon raises questions about the efficacy of the American political system in responding to complex challenges, especially when compared to the more consensus-driven approaches observed in many European democracies.

Political parties in the U.S. also play a vital role in shaping public policy through their influence on legislative agendas and governance. The party in power typically sets the tone for policy initiatives, reflecting its ideological commitments and priorities. This process is further complicated by the checks and balances inherent in the U.S. political system, where executive, legislative, and judicial branches interact. The dominance of political parties in framing policy debates can lead to significant variances in public policy outcomes between administrations, demonstrating the power wielded by party organizations in shaping the direction of national discourse.

Examining the role of political parties across the Atlantic underscores critical lessons for both American and European political landscapes. The contrasting party systems reveal different approaches to representation and governance, highlighting the advantages and challenges inherent in each model. By analyzing these differences, political actors and citizens can glean insights into enhancing democratic practices, fostering political engagement, and ultimately bridging the divides that characterize contemporary political life. The comparative analysis of political parties not only enriches our understanding of their roles in shaping public policy but also opens avenues for meaningful dialogue about future political cooperation and reform.

ELECTORAL SYSTEMS AND POLITICAL REPRESENTATION

OVERVIEW OF EUROPEAN ELECTORAL SYSTEMS

Electoral systems in Europe vary significantly across the continent, reflecting diverse political traditions, historical contexts, and societal values. Broadly speaking, European countries employ either proportional representation or majoritarian systems, with many nations favoring proportional representation to ensure that a wider array of political parties can compete and gain representation in legislative bodies. This contrasts sharply with the predominantly winner-takes-all, majoritarian system found in the United States, which often leads to a two-party system. The differences in these electoral systems have profound implications for political representation, shaping the nature of party competition and the overall political landscape in each region.

In many European countries, proportional representation allows for a multiplicity of parties, which can lead to coalition governments. This system encourages smaller parties to participate in the political process, ensuring that diverse viewpoints are represented in governance. For instance, nations like Sweden and the Netherlands have robust multi-party systems where coalitions are the norm, requiring political parties to work together to form stable governments. This contrasts with the U.S. system, where the dominance of the two major parties often stifles competition and marginalizes alternative voices, leading to a more binary political discourse that can alienate voters seeking different options.

The impact of these electoral systems on political representation is further illustrated when examining voter turnout and public engagement. European nations generally exhibit higher voter turnout rates compared to the United States, which can be attributed to several factors, including the accessibility of the electoral process and the perceived relevance of multiple parties to voters' interests. Countries such as Belgium and Denmark boast turnout rates exceeding 80 percent, reflecting a political culture that values participation and representation. In contrast, the U.S. struggles with turnout rates around 60 percent in presidential elections and significantly lower numbers in midterms, illustrating a disconnect between the electorate and the limited options presented by a two-party system.

Examining the role of political parties in shaping public policy reveals another layer of complexity in the transatlantic comparison. In Europe, political parties often have strong ideological foundations that guide their policy platforms, leading to more cohesive and predictable policy agendas. This enables parties to mobilize support around specific issues, such as environmental policy or social welfare, in a way that resonates with their constituents. In the U.S., the fluidity of party platforms can result in less predictable governance outcomes, as parties may shift their positions in response to electoral pressures or changes in public opinion, creating challenges for long-term policy planning and implementation.

Historical context also plays a crucial role in shaping contemporary political ideologies across Europe and the U.S. The legacy of post-war reconstruction in Europe and the establishment of welfare states set the stage for a political landscape that prioritizes social equity and collective responsibility. In contrast, American political ideology has often emphasized individualism and limited government intervention. This divergence has influenced not only electoral systems but also the nature of populist movements and the framing of immigration policies. As both regions grapple with issues of representation and governance, understanding these foundational differences provides valuable insights for bridging the divide and fostering transatlantic dialogue on key political challenges.

The U.S Electoral System: A Critical Examination

The United States electoral system, characterized by its unique combination of federalism and a predominantly two-party structure, presents a distinctive paradigm when compared to European models. The system is built around a winner-takes-all approach in most elections, particularly for the House of Representatives and the presidency. This creates significant barriers for third parties and independents, often leading to a political landscape dominated by the Democratic and Republican parties. The implications of this electoral framework extend beyond mere party competition; they shape the broader political culture and influence voter engagement, policy formulation, and the nature of political discourse across the nation.

In contrast, many European countries employ proportional representation systems, which allow for a wider array of political parties to participate in governance. This inclusion leads to coalition governments, fostering a more pluralistic political environment. The European model often facilitates the representation of diverse political ideologies, including those on the fringes of the mainstream. Consequently, European political parties tend to be more responsive to a broader spectrum of public opinion, enabling them to address issues that might be overlooked in a more polarized American system. This divergence invites critical questions about the efficacy of political representation and the legitimacy of governance in both contexts.

The role of political parties in shaping public policy further illuminates the differences between the US and European systems. In the US, the two dominant parties often prioritize short-term electoral gains, leading to policy decisions that can be reactive rather than proactive. This is exacerbated by the influence of money in politics, which can skew priorities toward the interests of wealthy donors over the general populace. In contrast, European parties often operate within frameworks that encourage long-term planning and collaboration, promoting policies that address systemic issues such as climate change, social welfare, and economic inequality. The structural incentives of the electoral system play a crucial role in determining whether political parties can act as effective agents of change or if they become mired in partisan conflict.

Moreover, the historical context of the US and Europe has significantly influenced contemporary political ideologies and movements. The legacy of the New Deal, the civil rights movement, and recent populist trends reflect a distinctly American narrative that contrasts sharply with European experiences of social democracy and welfare state evolution. Populism, in particular, has manifested differently across the Atlantic, with US movements often focusing on nationalism and anti-establishment sentiments, while European populism may intertwine with issues of immigration and technocracy. This divergence provides a rich ground for comparative political analysis, revealing how historical legacies shape present-day ideologies and party platforms.

Ultimately, examining the US electoral system through a critical lens reveals not only its limitations but also opportunities for reform. By learning from European approaches to political representation, the United States could explore alternatives that promote greater inclusivity and responsiveness in governance. The transatlantic dialogue around electoral systems invites a reconsideration of existing frameworks, challenging the binary nature of American politics and opening pathways for a more representative democracy. Such an examination highlights the potential for bridging divides, fostering cooperation, and enriching political discourse on both sides of the Atlantic.

PUBLIC POLICY AND POLITICAL PARTIES

POLICY DEVELOPMENT IN EUROPEAN CONTEXTS

Policy development in European contexts presents a rich complexity of approaches that differ significantly from those in the United States. European nations often navigate their political landscapes through a blend of historical legacies, cultural values, and institutional frameworks that prioritize social welfare and collective governance. This contrasts sharply with the more individualistic and market-oriented approach seen in the U.S. The emphasis on consensus-building and coalition politics in many European countries fosters a unique environment for policy innovation, allowing for a broader spectrum of political dialogue that can accommodate a variety of perspectives.

One of the notable advantages of European policy development is its capacity for comprehensive welfare state models, which vary from country to country but generally prioritize social safety nets and public goods. Nations such as Sweden and Germany exemplify how robust welfare policies can address socioeconomic disparities and promote social cohesion. In contrast, the U.S. welfare system is often criticized for its fragmented nature, which can leave vulnerable populations without adequate support. This comparative analysis underscores the lessons that American policymakers might glean from European models, particularly in the areas of healthcare, education, and social services.

The electoral systems in Europe further illustrate how political representation is achieved differently compared to the U.S. Many European countries employ proportional representation, which allows for a wider range of political parties and voices within their parliaments. This system can lead to more inclusive governance, as smaller parties often have a seat at the table, reflecting a multitude of viewpoints. In the United States, the winner-takes-all electoral system tends to favor two dominant parties, often marginalizing alternative perspectives and leading to heightened political polarization. Understanding these structural differences is crucial for analyzing how policies are crafted and implemented in each context.

Political parties play a pivotal role in shaping public policy across the Atlantic, acting as gatekeepers to the political discourse and influencing the legislative agenda. In Europe, parties often have clear ideological identities that resonate with specific demographic groups, allowing for targeted policy initiatives that address their constituents' needs. This contrasts with the more centrist tendencies often observed in U.S. parties, which may dilute distinct ideological positions in an effort to appeal to a broader electorate. The dynamics within political parties can thus significantly impact policy outcomes, highlighting the importance of party structure and strategy in both contexts.

Finally, the influence of historical context on contemporary political ideologies cannot be overstated. European nations have been shaped by diverse historical experiences, including revolutions, wars, and the evolution of the European Union, which have profoundly affected their political landscapes. These historical narratives foster a sense of collective identity that influences policy priorities, such as environmental sustainability and social equity. In the U.S., a different historical trajectory, marked by ideals of individualism and limited government intervention, has shaped its political ideologies. By examining these historical contexts, one can better understand the current political movements, including the rise of populism and the challenges of governance amidst increasing polarization in both Europe and the United States.

The Influence *of* Political Parties *on* U.S Policy

Political parties play a crucial role in shaping public policy in the United States, influencing everything from healthcare and education to environmental regulations and economic policy. The two dominant parties, the Democrats and Republicans, embody differing ideologies and priorities that reflect their historical contexts and constituencies. This duality shapes not only electoral outcomes but also the legislative agenda, as each party seeks to implement its vision for the country. The influence of political parties is further compounded by the American electoral system, which, unlike many European systems, is characterized by a winner-takes-all approach that often marginalizes third parties and alternative political movements.

In the U.S., the political landscape has become increasingly polarized, with parties retreating further into their ideological corners. This polarization influences how policies are developed and enacted, often leading to gridlock in Congress. The historical context of this division can be traced to various factors, including the civil rights movement, economic disparities, and cultural shifts. As parties align themselves more closely with specific interest groups and demographic segments, their ability to enact bipartisan policies diminishes, resulting in a political environment where compromise is increasingly rare. This dynamic contrasts sharply with some European countries, where coalition governments necessitate negotiation and collaboration among multiple parties.

Examining the comparative analysis of welfare state models reveals significant differences between the U.S. and European approaches. In Europe, many political parties advocate for expansive welfare policies, reflecting a societal commitment to social safety nets and public services. In contrast, U.S. political parties are often divided on the extent of government intervention in the economy, with Republicans typically favoring limited government and Democrats advocating for more robust social programs. This divergence in welfare philosophy not only affects legislation but also shapes public discourse surrounding issues such as healthcare, education, and unemployment benefits, highlighting a fundamental ideological divide across the Atlantic.

The role of political parties extends beyond domestic policy, influencing international relations and the perception of global issues. For instance, environmental policy in the U.S. has been significantly impacted by party affiliation, with Democrats generally supporting more aggressive climate action compared to their Republican counterparts. This divergence presents an opportunity for European countries to share best practices and policy frameworks that have proven effective in addressing environmental challenges. By examining these differences, U.S. political parties can learn from European models and potentially reshape their approaches to sustainability and climate change.

The implications of political parties on immigration policies reveal another area of divergence. In the U.S., immigration remains a contentious issue, with political parties adopting starkly different stances that reflect broader ideological beliefs about national identity and economic opportunity. Meanwhile, Europe grapples with its own complex immigration challenges, shaped by historical context and regional dynamics. By analyzing these different approaches, political parties on both sides of the Atlantic can gain valuable insights into crafting policies that address public concerns while respecting humanitarian obligations. Ultimately, understanding the influence of political parties on policy can foster greater dialogue and collaboration, bridging divides and enhancing mutual understanding across the Atlantic.

HISTORICAL CONTEXT AND IDEOLOGICAL DEVELOPMENT

THE EVOLUTION OF POLITICAL IDEOLOGIES IN EUROPE

The evolution of political ideologies in Europe has been shaped by a complex interplay of historical events, cultural shifts, and socio-economic transformations. Beginning with the Enlightenment, ideas of democracy, individual rights, and social contract theory laid the groundwork for modern political thought. This intellectual awakening fueled revolutions and reform movements across the continent, notably the French Revolution, which not only inspired political change in France but also influenced revolutionary movements in other parts of Europe and beyond. The emergence of liberalism and its subsequent challenges from socialism and conservatism reflected the diverse responses to industrialization and changing social structures.

The 20th century saw the rise of totalitarian regimes and the subsequent establishment of democratic states in the post-World War II landscape. The ideological battle between communism and capitalism during the Cold War further polarized European political thought, leading to the formation of distinct political blocs. In Western Europe, the welfare state emerged as a response to the economic crises of the interwar years, promoting a blend of social democratic principles that aimed to balance free-market capitalism with social equity. This model established a framework for political ideologies focused on social justice, public welfare, and the role of the state in mitigating inequalities, contrasting sharply with the more individualistic approach predominant in the United States.

The late 20th and early 21st centuries have witnessed a resurgence of populism across Europe, challenging established political parties and traditional ideologies. This shift can be attributed to a growing disillusionment with globalization and its perceived failures to address local concerns, such as economic insecurity and cultural identity. Populist movements have capitalized on these sentiments, often employing nationalist rhetoric that resonates with segments of the population feeling left behind by mainstream politics. Understanding these transatlantic populist trends is essential for analyzing how political ideologies have evolved in response to contemporary challenges, highlighting the differences and similarities between European and American experiences.

In examining the role of political parties in shaping public policy, it is evident that European parties often operate within a multiparty system, leading to coalition governments that necessitate compromise and negotiation. This contrasts with the predominantly two-party system in the United States, where partisan polarization often results in gridlock. The European experience shows how diverse political representation can lead to more inclusive policy-making processes, while the U.S. model highlights the challenges of achieving consensus amid increasing ideological divides. Both systems provide valuable lessons in governance, particularly regarding the impact of electoral systems on political representation and the broader implications for democratic engagement.

Finally, the historical context of political ideologies in Europe continues to inform contemporary debates around issues such as immigration, environmental policy, and gender representation. The European Union's role as a supranational organization has facilitated collaboration on these issues, providing a platform for collective action that contrasts with the often fragmented approach seen in U.S. politics. By analyzing these developments, one can appreciate the nuances of European political ideologies and their implications for transatlantic relationships. Understanding these dynamics is crucial for fostering dialogue and cooperation between Europe and the United States, as both regions navigate the complexities of modern governance in an increasingly interconnected world.

Contemporary Political Ideologies *in the* U.S

Contemporary political ideologies in the United States are characterized by a complex interplay of traditional values, emerging movements, and responses to global challenges. The political landscape is primarily dominated by two major parties: the Democratic Party, which leans toward liberalism and social democracy, and the Republican Party, which encompasses conservatism and libertarianism. Each party reflects a distinct set of beliefs about the role of government, individual rights, and the distribution of resources, which are shaped by historical contexts and current societal needs. The ideological divide is not merely a matter of policy preference but is deeply rooted in contrasting visions for the future of the nation, influenced by diverse constituencies and their varying priorities.

A comparative analysis of welfare state models in Europe and the United States reveals significant differences in how each system addresses social needs. European countries typically adopt a more expansive welfare state approach, emphasizing universal healthcare, education, and social security as fundamental rights. In contrast, the U.S. welfare system is more fragmented and often viewed through the lens of individual responsibility. This divergence reflects broader ideological beliefs about government intervention and the perceived role of the state in ensuring the well-being of its citizens. As contemporary issues such as healthcare access and income inequality gain prominence, the U.S. may find valuable lessons in European models that prioritize social equity while also fostering economic growth.

Electoral systems across the Atlantic further shape political representation and party dynamics. The United States employs a winner-takes-all system that often leads to a two-party structure, potentially marginalizing smaller parties and independent candidates. In contrast, many European nations utilize proportional representation, which encourages a multi-party system and allows for a broader spectrum of political ideologies to be represented in government. This difference affects not only the types of policies that emerge but also how citizens engage with the political process, fostering a more inclusive dialogue in Europe while prompting calls for electoral reform in the U.S. to enhance representation and reduce polarization.

The rise of populism, both in Europe and the U.S., highlights a shared reaction against established political norms and institutions. Populist movements often draw on discontent with traditional parties, economic insecurity, and cultural anxieties, framing their narratives around the notion of a "true" people versus a detached elite. While the specific manifestations of populism may differ—such as the right-wing populism seen in parts of Europe or left-leaning populist movements in the U.S.—the underlying sentiments reveal a collective yearning for change and a disconnect from conventional political discourse. These movements pose significant challenges to governance and require careful examination of their implications for democratic stability.

Contemporary political ideologies in the U.S. are also influenced by pressing global issues such as environmental policy and immigration. American political discourse often contrasts sharply with European approaches, where environmental regulations are typically more stringent, reflecting a broader consensus on climate change as a critical priority. Similarly, immigration policies reveal ideological divides, with European countries grappling with integration while the U.S. debates border security and the role of immigrants in society. Understanding these ideological differences is crucial for fostering a transatlantic dialogue that can bridge divides, share best practices, and promote collaborative solutions to shared challenges. As political landscapes evolve, the lessons learned from each side of the Atlantic will be essential for addressing the complexities of contemporary governance.

POPULISM ACROSS THE ATLANTIC

THE RISE OF POPULIST MOVEMENTS IN EUROPE

The rise of populist movements in Europe has emerged as a significant phenomenon in the contemporary political landscape, reflecting broader shifts in societal attitudes and political engagement. Rooted in a discontent with traditional political institutions, these movements have gained traction by appealing to the emotions and frustrations of various demographics. In many cases, they have been fueled by economic disparities, cultural anxieties, and a perceived disconnect between the political elite and the everyday concerns of citizens. This populist wave has challenged established political parties, prompting a reassessment of political representation and accountability in Europe.

Populism often thrives in environments characterized by economic uncertainty and social change. In Europe, the aftermath of the 2008 financial crisis laid the groundwork for many populist parties to emerge. These parties capitalized on the growing disillusionment with austerity measures and the perceived failures of traditional parties to address the needs of ordinary people. By framing themselves as champions of the "common folk" against the elite, these movements have managed to attract a diverse base, including those who feel marginalized by globalization and rapid demographic changes. The electoral success of parties like the National Rally in France and the Alternative for Germany illustrates how populism can disrupt the political status quo.

The impact of populist movements on European political dynamics cannot be overstated. They have not only influenced national elections but have also reshaped the discourse around critical issues such as immigration, national identity, and social welfare. Populist leaders often advocate for stricter immigration controls and a return to national sovereignty, positioning themselves against the European Union's supranational governance. This has led to heightened tensions within the EU and raised questions about the future of European integration. As populist parties gain seats in parliaments, their presence forces traditional parties to reconsider their platforms and electoral strategies.

Comparative analysis reveals that the rise of populism in Europe offers valuable lessons for the United States. While the contexts may differ, both regions share a growing sentiment of discontent with established political structures. In the US, similar populist sentiments have emerged, leading to significant electoral outcomes and policy debates. The examination of these movements across the Atlantic highlights the importance of understanding the underlying factors that contribute to populism, such as economic inequality and cultural polarization. By analyzing the European experience, American political actors may identify strategies to address the root causes of populism before it further polarizes their own political landscape.

Ultimately, the rise of populist movements in Europe serves as a critical reminder of the need for political parties to adapt to changing public sentiments. As these movements continue to challenge traditional political norms, the implications for public policy and governance are profound. The need to engage citizens in meaningful dialogue, address economic disparities, and foster inclusive political representation is paramount. Bridging the divide between populist sentiments and established political frameworks is essential not only for European stability but also for fostering a more cohesive transatlantic relationship in an increasingly interconnected world.

Understanding Populism *in the* U.S

Populism in the United States has surged to the forefront of contemporary politics, a potent force defined by its fervent appeal to the "common people" in opposition to a perceived corrupt and self-serving elite. This phenomenon, fueled by deep-seated discontent among various segments of society, particularly those who feel marginalized by economic shifts and political decisions, is not entirely new. The roots of American populism can be traced back to agrarian movements of the late 19th century and the progressive era, but in recent years, it has gained unprecedented visibility and influence, reshaping party dynamics, altering public discourse, and posing fundamental questions about the nature of democratic governance. By understanding the underlying causes, diverse manifestations, and potential long-term consequences of populism in the U.S., one can better appreciate its implications in the broader context of transatlantic relations and the global rise of similar movements.

At the heart of U.S. populism lies a palpable reaction to economic inequality and the perceived failures of globalization. For decades, many Americans have experienced stagnant wages, declining job security, and a widening gap between the rich and the poor. This economic frustration has been exacerbated by the outsourcing of jobs, the rise of automation, and the concentration of wealth in the hands of a few. This has led to a pervasive sense of betrayal by traditional political institutions, which are often seen as beholden to corporate interests and out of touch with the struggles of ordinary citizens. In this fertile ground, populist leaders often position themselves as champions of the "forgotten man" or "common woman," promising to dismantle the perceived status quo, drain the swamp of corruption, and restore power to the people. This resonant narrative cuts across various demographics, including white working-class voters, rural communities, and those disillusioned with established parties, revealing the multifaceted and often contradictory nature of populist appeal. The rise of digital media and social networks has further amplified these sentiments, allowing individuals to connect with like-minded individuals, bypass traditional gatekeepers of information, and organize politically around shared grievances.

Comparatively, European populism shares several traits with its American counterpart, including a distrust of elites, a focus on national identity, and a critique of globalization. However, it also reflects distinct historical, cultural, and political contexts. In Europe, populist movements often capitalize on anxieties surrounding national identity, immigration, and the perceived erosion of national sovereignty by the European Union. While U.S. populism frequently emphasizes economic grievances and the promise of economic nationalism, European variants may place a greater emphasis on cultural anxieties related to immigration, integration, and the preservation of traditional values. The legacy of colonialism, the experience of large-scale immigration flows, and the supranational structures of the EU have all shaped the specific contours of populism on the continent. This divergence highlights the importance of contextual factors in shaping populist agendas and underscores the idea that lessons learned from one region may not be directly translatable to another. By carefully examining these similarities and differences, observers can gain a more nuanced understanding of how populism operates within a variety of political frameworks and how it interacts with existing social and economic cleavages.

The role of political parties in the United States has been significantly impacted by the rise of populism, leading to shifts in traditional party alignments, electoral strategies, and the very definition of what it means to be a Democrat or a Republican. Established parties, particularly the Democrats and Republicans, have had to grapple with the challenge of accommodating or countering populist sentiments within their bases. This has led to internal divisions, ideological clashes, and the emergence of new factions that prioritize populist ideals over traditional party platforms. For example, the election of Donald Trump as president in 2016 demonstrated the power of populist rhetoric to mobilize voters and disrupt established political norms. His presidency exposed deep divisions within the Republican party and led to a reassessment of the party's core values and priorities. Similarly, the rise of Bernie Sanders within the Democratic party highlighted the growing appeal of socialist ideas and the desire for a more progressive economic agenda. These dynamics pose fundamental questions about the future of political representation in the U.S. and the potential for populist movements to reshape party politics in the coming years, reflecting a broader trend observed in Europe as well, where traditional party systems have been challenged by the rise of populist parties on both the left and the right. The ability of established parties to adapt to these changing political landscapes will be crucial for maintaining their relevance and legitimacy in the years to come.

The impact of populism extends beyond domestic politics and significantly shapes the United States' relationships with its transatlantic partners. Populist leaders often adopt an "America First" approach to foreign policy, prioritizing national interests over multilateral cooperation and international agreements. This can lead to tensions with allies, trade disputes, and a weakening of international institutions. In Europe, the rise of populist movements has similarly led to calls for greater national sovereignty, skepticism towards the EU, and a more protectionist approach to trade. These trends can strain transatlantic relations and create new challenges for cooperation on issues such as climate change, security, and global governance. However, they also create an opportunity for dialogue and collaboration, as both the U.S. and Europe grapple with similar challenges related to economic inequality, social division, and the future of democracy.

Understanding populism in the United States requires a comprehensive approach that considers both its domestic implications and its transatlantic connections. By analyzing the complex interplay between economic factors, cultural identity, political representation, and technological change, one can begin to grasp how populism has influenced not only U.S. governance but also its relationships with European counterparts. As both regions navigate the challenges posed by populism, there is a unique opportunity for cross-Atlantic dialogue, shared learning, and the development of innovative solutions that may provide valuable insights into fostering more inclusive, representative, and resilient political systems. This dialogue should focus on addressing the root causes of populism, promoting economic opportunity for all, strengthening democratic institutions, and fostering a sense of shared identity and purpose. Only through a concerted effort can we hope to overcome the challenges posed by populism and build a more just and equitable world for future generations.

POLITICAL POLARIZATION AND GOVERNANCE

THE EFFECTS OF POLARIZATION IN EUROPE

The effects of polarization in Europe manifest in a variety of ways, deeply influencing political discourse, governance, and public policy. As political parties become increasingly divided along ideological lines, the capacity for consensus-building diminishes. This erosion of collaborative dialogue hampers the ability of governments to address pressing issues such as climate change, social welfare, and immigration. In contrast to the often binary polarization seen in the United States, European polarization can take on multifaceted forms, with multiple parties representing a spectrum of ideologies. This complexity can lead to fragmented parliaments, making it difficult for any single party to secure a governing majority, thus necessitating coalition-building that complicates policy implementation.

The rise of populism in Europe serves as a critical response to this polarization, mirroring trends observed in the U.S. political landscape. Populist parties, often characterized by their anti-establishment rhetoric, have gained traction by capitalizing on the discontent among voters who feel alienated by traditional political elites. This phenomenon has led to a significant reshaping of political alliances and has forced established parties to reevaluate their platforms. The emergence of these movements raises questions about the future of democratic governance in Europe, as they challenge the established norms of political discourse and policy formulation. Consequently, the increasing influence of populism can further entrench divisions, making it even more challenging to forge common ground on key issues.

In examining the electoral systems across Europe and the U.S., one finds that the effects of polarization are not uniform. European systems, often characterized by proportional representation, allow for a wider range of voices and perspectives in the political arena. This inclusivity can both mitigate and exacerbate polarization. While it provides opportunities for minority parties to gain representation, it can also lead to a proliferation of parties that complicate governance. In contrast, the winner-takes-all approach in the U.S. tends to exacerbate polarization by marginalizing third parties and reinforcing a binary political landscape. The implications of these different systems on political representation are profound, influencing voter engagement and the overall health of democracy on both sides of the Atlantic.

Moreover, the historical context of European countries contributes significantly to contemporary political ideologies and polarization. The legacy of conflicts, colonialism, and differing economic models has shaped the political narratives within various nations. For instance, countries with strong social democratic traditions often prioritize welfare state models, which can be at odds with neoliberal policies prevalent in other parts of Europe and the U.S. This divergence in values can intensify polarization, as parties align themselves with specific historical narratives that resonate with their constituents. Understanding these historical influences is essential for grasping the complexities of current political dynamics and the challenges faced by policymakers in bridging divides.

The impact of political polarization on governance in Europe is a pressing concern that warrants careful consideration. The ability of governments to effectively address critical issues such as environmental policy, gender representation, and immigration is often compromised by entrenched divisions. As European nations grapple with the ramifications of polarization, lessons can be drawn for the U.S., particularly regarding the importance of collaborative governance and the need for political parties to engage in constructive dialogue. By fostering a political culture that values compromise and inclusivity, both

Europe and the U.S. can work towards a more cohesive and effective approach to governance that benefits all citizens.

Political Polarization *in the* US: Causes *and* Consequences

Political polarization in the United States has become a defining characteristic of its political landscape, manifesting in increasing partisanship and ideological divides. Several factors contribute to this phenomenon, including the role of social media, the influence of partisan news outlets, and the strategic decisions made by political parties themselves. Social media platforms often create echo chambers, where users are exposed predominantly to information that reinforces their preexisting beliefs. This selective exposure exacerbates divisions, making it increasingly difficult for individuals to engage with opposing viewpoints. Furthermore, the proliferation of partisan news sources has led to a fragmented media environment, where the lines between fact and opinion are blurred, further entrenching polarized positions.

The consequences of political polarization extend beyond mere ideological differences; they have profound implications for governance and public policy. In a highly polarized environment, compromise becomes increasingly elusive, resulting in legislative gridlock. Political parties prioritize party loyalty over bipartisan cooperation, leading to a situation where essential issues such as healthcare, education, and immigration remain unresolved. This gridlock not only frustrates citizens who seek effective governance but also undermines public trust in democratic institutions. As parties become more extreme in their positions, the space for moderate voices diminishes, contributing to an overall decline in political discourse.

Comparatively, the political polarization observed in the United States contrasts sharply with many European countries, where coalition governments and proportional representation systems encourage more inclusive political dialogue. In several European democracies, the presence of multiple political parties allows for a wider range of perspectives and fosters collaboration among diverse ideological groups. This structural difference often leads to more stable governance and a focus on consensus-building rather than adversarial politics. By examining these contrasting electoral systems, it becomes evident that the design of political institutions plays a crucial role in shaping the nature of political engagement and representation.

Historical context also plays a significant role in understanding contemporary political ideologies in both regions. The United States has a unique political history characterized by strong individualism and a two-party system that has evolved from its founding principles. In contrast, many European countries developed welfare states in response to historical crises, such as World War II, leading to a stronger emphasis on social solidarity and collective responsibility. This divergence in historical trajectories influences how citizens perceive issues such as immigration, environmental policy, and gender representation, shaping their political affiliations and the platforms of political parties.

Finally, the rise of populism on both sides of the Atlantic illustrates the ramifications of political polarization. In the U.S., populist movements have capitalized on discontent with the political establishment, further deepening divisions. Similarly, in Europe, populist parties have gained traction by appealing to nationalist sentiments, often in opposition to supranational entities like the European Union. These movements not only challenge traditional political norms but also highlight the need for a reevaluation of political strategies that bridge divides. By learning from each other's experiences, both the United States and Europe can gain valuable insights into addressing polarization and fostering a more constructive political environment.

THE ROLE OF SUPRANATIONAL ORGANIZATIONS

THE EUROPEAN UNION AND ITS INFLUENCE

The European Union (EU) stands as a remarkable example of regional cooperation and integration, significantly influencing both domestic and international political landscapes. Established in the wake of World War II, the EU aims to foster peace, stability, and economic collaboration among its member states. This political entity not only promotes economic ties but also serves as a platform for addressing shared challenges, such as climate change, security threats, and migration. Its influence extends beyond Europe, shaping policies and political discourses in the United States and other regions. The EU's policies and regulatory frameworks, particularly in areas like environmental standards and social welfare, provide valuable lessons for the U.S. as it navigates its own complex political landscape.

One of the most striking distinctions between the EU and the U.S. lies in their approaches to welfare state models. European nations generally embrace a more extensive welfare state, characterized by comprehensive social safety nets and universal healthcare systems. This is often contrasted with the U.S. model, which tends to favor a more market-oriented approach. The EU's experience with welfare policies highlights the potential benefits of prioritizing social equity and inclusion, offering insights into how the U.S. might address its own socioeconomic disparities. By examining these models, political leaders and policymakers in the U.S. can glean lessons on balancing economic efficiency with social responsibility.

Electoral systems play a crucial role in shaping political representation across the Atlantic. Many European countries employ proportional representation, which tends to create multi-party systems that allow for a wider range of political voices. In contrast, the U.S. predominantly uses a winner-takes-all system, often resulting in a two-party dominance that can marginalize alternative viewpoints. This difference in electoral systems has profound implications for political engagement, voter representation, and the overall health of democracy. Understanding these dynamics is essential for fostering a more inclusive political discourse in the U.S., particularly in light of rising populist movements that challenge traditional party structures.

The historical context of both regions also significantly influences contemporary political ideologies. Europe's political landscape is deeply rooted in its past, shaped by experiences such as colonialism, two world wars, and the Cold War. These factors have cultivated a political environment that values collective identity and social cohesion. In contrast, the U.S. has a history of individualism and a frontier mentality, which continues to inform its political ideologies. Analyzing these historical narratives reveals how they contribute to current political polarization and public sentiment, providing a framework for understanding the challenges faced by both regions in fostering effective governance.

In addressing pressing global issues such as environmental policy and immigration, the EU has often taken a proactive stance that contrasts with U.S. practices. European countries typically prioritize sustainability and climate action, driving ambitious policies that set examples for global standards. Conversely, U.S. policies on these issues have varied widely, often influenced by political polarization and differing public opinions. The EU's commitment to environmental responsibility can serve as a model for U.S. political discourse, encouraging a shift toward more sustainable practices. Similarly, the EU's approach to immigration, which emphasizes human rights and integration, offers critical insights into addressing the complexities of migration in a manner that promotes social harmony. By learning from Europe's experiences, the U.S. can better navigate its own political challenges, fostering a more inclusive and effective governance model.

Implications *for* US Relations *with* Europe

The implications for US relations with Europe are multifaceted, particularly when considering the contrasting political paradigms that shape each region. The United States, with its individualistic approach and federal system, often stands in stark contrast to the more collectivist tendencies observed in various European nations. This divergence in political philosophy affects not only domestic policies but also international relations. As Europe grapples with issues such as immigration and economic disparity through welfare state models, the US must navigate these complexities to foster a more cooperative relationship. Understanding these differences is crucial for US policymakers seeking to bridge the Atlantic divide and forge a path forward that respects diverse perspectives while addressing shared global challenges.

The foundation of these divergent political landscapes lies in fundamentally different understandings of the role of government and the relationship between the individual and the state. In the US, a strong emphasis on individual liberty and limited government intervention has historically shaped policy debates. This is reflected in a preference for market-based solutions and a skepticism towards expansive social safety nets. Conversely, many European nations have embraced a more interventionist role for the state in providing social welfare, healthcare, and education. This difference stems from distinct historical trajectories, with Europe experiencing the rise of social democracy and labor movements that advocated for a robust public sector. The US, on the other hand, has traditionally emphasized self-reliance and entrepreneurialism. This contrast in values and priorities often translates into disagreements on issues ranging from trade regulations and environmental policy to international security and humanitarian aid.

A comparative analysis of electoral systems reveals significant differences between Europe and the US, which has profound implications for political representation. European countries often utilize proportional representation, allowing for a wider array of political parties and perspectives in governance. In contrast, the US primarily employs a winner-takes-all system that tends to favor the two-party landscape. This distinction shapes public policy development and responsiveness to citizens' needs. The proportional representation systems in Europe often lead to coalition governments, requiring parties to compromise and negotiate to form a governing majority. This can result in more inclusive and representative policies that reflect the diverse interests of the electorate. However, it can also lead to political instability and gridlock, as coalition governments are often fragile and prone to infighting. The winner-takes-all system in the US, while promoting political stability and clear lines of accountability, can marginalize minority voices and lead to policy outcomes that disproportionately favor the interests of the dominant parties. As political polarization increases in both regions, recognizing the impact of these electoral systems can inform strategies for enhancing transatlantic cooperation and mutual understanding. Exploring the potential for electoral reforms that promote greater inclusivity and representation could be a valuable avenue for strengthening democratic institutions on both sides of the Atlantic.

Political parties play a pivotal role in shaping public policy across the Atlantic, and their influence varies significantly between Europe and the US. In many European systems, political parties are more ideologically cohesive and often form coalitions to govern, which can lead to more comprehensive policy solutions that reflect diverse viewpoints. The stronger party discipline in Europe often allows for the implementation of more ambitious policy agendas compared to the US.

Furthermore, the multi-party systems encourage a broader range of viewpoints to be considered in the policy-making process. Conversely, the US political landscape is marked by a two-party system wherein party loyalty can obstruct bipartisan cooperation. The increasing polarization of the two major parties in the US has made it increasingly difficult to find common ground on critical issues, leading to legislative gridlock and a perception of government dysfunction. This dynamic complicates transatlantic dialogue, particularly on pressing issues like environmental policy, trade agreements, and security cooperation. By examining the role of political parties in both regions, stakeholders can identify best practices for enhancing collaboration and addressing shared challenges. Facilitating exchanges between political leaders and party strategists from the US and Europe could foster a deeper understanding of each other's political systems and promote more effective collaboration on issues of mutual concern.

The historical context of both regions heavily influences contemporary political ideologies, shaping attitudes toward governance and policy-making. Europe's history of social democracy and welfare state development contrasts sharply with the US's emphasis on free-market principles and limited government intervention. The legacy of the World Wars and the subsequent development of the European Union has fostered a sense of collective responsibility and international cooperation among many European nations. This historical experience has shaped their approach to foreign policy and their commitment to multilateral institutions. In contrast, the US has historically viewed itself as a global leader, often acting unilaterally in pursuit of its national interests. These historical narratives not only inform public opinion but also affect how each region approaches global issues, such as climate change and economic inequality. The US's initial reluctance to fully embrace the Paris Climate Agreement, for example, reflects a deeper skepticism towards international agreements and a greater emphasis on national sovereignty. Understanding these historical influences is crucial for navigating the transatlantic relationship. By acknowledging the different historical experiences that have shaped their political cultures, US relations with Europe can be recalibrated to improve diplomatic efforts and foster a more unified approach to global challenges. This includes recognizing the value of multilateralism and the importance of addressing global issues through cooperative frameworks.

The rise of populism in both Europe and the US sheds light on the shifting political landscape and its implications for transatlantic relations. Populist movements often capitalize on grievances related to globalization, economic disparity, and cultural identity, leading to increased political polarization. These movements often challenge established political norms and institutions, leading to instability and uncertainty in the political landscape. In Europe, populist parties have gained significant traction by tapping into anxieties about immigration, cultural change, and European integration. In the US, populism has manifested in the form of economic nationalism and a rejection of globalization. This phenomenon can strain diplomatic ties, as divergent responses to populism can exacerbate misunderstandings. The rise of nationalist sentiment and protectionist policies in both regions can undermine transatlantic trade and cooperation. Differing approaches to immigration policy and border control can also create tensions between the US and Europe. By adopting a transatlantic perspective on these political movements, both regions can better navigate the complexities of their relationship, fostering dialogue that addresses common concerns while respecting diverse political contexts. This dialogue should focus on understanding the root causes of populism, addressing the concerns of marginalized communities, and promoting inclusive economic growth.

Ultimately, the future of US-European relations hinges on a willingness to understand and respect the diverse political cultures and historical experiences that shape each region. While differences will undoubtedly persist, a commitment to open dialogue, mutual understanding, and a shared vision for global cooperation can help to bridge the Atlantic divide and forge a stronger and more resilient partnership. This requires not only engaging with government officials and political leaders but also fostering people-to-people exchanges, educational programs, and cultural initiatives that promote greater understanding and empathy between the citizens of the US and Europe. By embracing a spirit of collaboration and seeking common ground on issues of shared concern, the US and Europe can continue to play a leading role in addressing the complex challenges facing the world today.

GENDER REPRESENTATION IN POLITICS

GENDER EQUALITY IN EUROPEAN POLITICAL PARTIES

Gender equality within European political parties presents a unique case study when compared to the political landscape of the United States. In many European countries, political parties have made concerted efforts to address gender disparities through various mechanisms, such as gender quotas and affirmative action policies. These measures have significantly increased the representation of women in political positions, leading to a more balanced political discourse. In contrast, U.S. political parties have traditionally struggled to implement similar strategies, resulting in lower female representation in both elected offices and party leadership roles.

The implementation of gender quotas in European political parties has been a transformative factor in promoting gender equality. Countries like Sweden and Norway have adopted strict quotas that mandate a certain percentage of candidates to be women, leading to notable increases in female legislative representation. This approach contrasts sharply with the U.S. system, where political parties operate without enforced quotas, often relying on the voluntary commitment of party leaders to promote gender diversity. The absence of such mandates has allowed for a slower progression toward gender parity, highlighting a significant difference in how both regions approach the issue.

Moreover, the cultural and historical contexts of gender roles in Europe and the U.S. have shaped the political landscape in ways that impact party dynamics. In many European nations, there is a long-standing tradition of progressive social policies that support gender equality, often rooted in post-World War II reconstruction efforts that prioritized social welfare and inclusion. Conversely, the U.S. political narrative has often emphasized individualism, which can complicate collective efforts toward gender equality within political parties. This divergence influences not only the representation of women but also the policies that parties promote regarding gender issues.

Political parties also play a crucial role in shaping public policy related to gender equality. In Europe, parties that emphasize gender equality tend to prioritize issues such as childcare, parental leave, and reproductive rights, reflecting a broader commitment to social welfare. These policies are often supported by a coalition of left-leaning parties, which advocate for a more inclusive political agenda. In the U.S., however, the political landscape is more polarized, with gender-related policies often becoming contentious issues that divide parties along ideological lines. This polarization can hinder progress on gender equality initiatives and limit the effectiveness of political parties in advocating for women's rights.

The transatlantic examination of gender representation in political parties reveals not only the successes of European models but also the challenges faced by U.S. parties in achieving similar outcomes. While Europe has made significant strides in integrating gender equality into the political framework, the U.S. continues to grapple with systemic barriers that impede progress. Understanding these differences provides valuable lessons for both regions as they strive to bridge the divide in political representation, ultimately fostering a more equitable political environment. The ongoing dialogue around gender issues in politics remains critical, shaping the future of democratic governance on both sides of the Atlantic.

The State *of* Gender Representation *in the* U.S

The state of gender representation in the United States exhibits a complex interplay of progress and challenges, particularly when compared to European counterparts. While the U.S. has made significant strides in gender representation within political spheres, the pace of change remains slow and uneven across different levels of government. Women currently hold a record number of seats in Congress, yet their representation still falls short of parity with men. In contrast, many European nations have implemented more aggressive policies, such as gender quotas, which have led to higher percentages of women in political offices. This disparity highlights the need for a deeper examination of the structural and cultural factors that influence gender representation on both sides of the Atlantic. It calls for a nuanced understanding of how historical legacies, institutional frameworks, and societal attitudes collectively shape the political landscape.

One of the critical factors contributing to the differences in gender representation is the electoral system. The U.S. employs a winner-takes-all electoral model, which often marginalizes minority voices, including those of women. This system can create significant barriers for female candidates, particularly in competitive districts where incumbents hold substantial advantages. Incumbency bias, coupled with the financial resources often required to run competitive campaigns, poses a significant obstacle for women seeking to enter politics. On the other hand, many European countries utilize proportional representation, allowing for a more equitable distribution of political power among various demographics, including gender. This system often involves multi-member districts where parties nominate lists of candidates, and seats are allocated based on the proportion of votes received. As a result, women in Europe tend to have greater access to political offices, which fosters environments where diverse perspectives can influence policymaking. The shift towards proportional representation can lead to more inclusive and reflective governance, which is often lacking in winner-takes-all systems.

Political parties play a pivotal role in shaping gender representation in both regions. In the U.S., while both major parties have made commitments to increase female representation, progress has often been hampered by internal party dynamics and funding disparities. The influence of money in American politics can disproportionately favor male candidates who often have established networks and access to larger donor bases. In contrast, European political parties frequently adopt gender parity as a core principle, integrating it into their platforms and candidate selection processes. This proactive approach not only enhances the visibility of women in politics but also encourages a broader cultural acceptance of female leadership. By analyzing how political parties in each context prioritize gender representation, one can discern the varying degrees of commitment to gender equity within political structures. Furthermore, the presence of women in party leadership positions often correlates with a greater emphasis on gender equality initiatives and policies.

The historical context of gender roles also significantly impacts contemporary political ideologies regarding representation. In the U.S., deeply rooted patriarchal norms and historical exclusion of women from political participation have contributed to ongoing challenges in achieving gender equity. The legacy of the suffrage movement and the long struggle for women's rights continue to resonate in contemporary political discourse. Conversely, many European nations have experienced different historical trajectories that have facilitated earlier advances in women's rights and representation. For instance, the impact of World War II, which saw women taking on traditionally male roles in the workforce, significantly altered societal perceptions of women's capabilities and contributions in some European countries. This divergence underscores the importance of understanding how historical narratives shape current political landscapes and influence the strategies employed to promote gender equality. Examining the specific historical events and social movements that have shaped gender roles in each region is crucial for understanding the present disparities.

Beyond these structural and historical factors, societal attitudes and cultural norms also play a crucial role. In the United States, traditional gender stereotypes continue to influence perceptions of women in leadership positions. Women often face scrutiny regarding their competence, ambition, and even their physical appearance, which can create additional barriers to political success. These biases can manifest in subtle ways, such as media coverage that focuses more on a female candidate's personal life than her policy positions. In contrast, some European societies exhibit a greater acceptance of women in leadership roles, which can translate into stronger support for female candidates. Education and media representation play a vital role in shaping these cultural norms and perceptions. Promoting positive and diverse portrayals of women in leadership can help to challenge stereotypes and foster a more inclusive political environment.

The intersectionality of gender with other identities, such as race, ethnicity, and socioeconomic status, further complicates the issue of representation. Women of color, for example, often face compounded barriers to political participation due to the combined effects of gender and racial discrimination. Addressing these intersectional challenges requires a more comprehensive and nuanced approach to promoting gender equity. Policies and initiatives must be tailored to meet the specific needs and experiences of diverse groups of women. This includes addressing issues such as access to education, healthcare, and economic opportunities.

Ultimately, addressing the state of gender representation in the U.S. requires a multi-faceted approach that draws lessons from successful European models. By examining the effectiveness of gender quotas, proportional representation, and party commitments to diversity, American political leaders and activists can develop strategies that not only enhance women's political participation but also enrich the democratic process as a whole. But beyond simply adopting policies, a fundamental shift in cultural attitudes and societal norms is necessary. This requires a concerted effort to challenge gender stereotypes, promote gender equality in education and the media, and create a more inclusive and supportive environment for women in politics. Bridging the divide between the U.S. and Europe in this regard offers a valuable opportunity to foster more inclusive political environments that reflect the diversity of the populace and promote equitable governance. This collaborative approach can lead to more effective policymaking, increased civic engagement, and a more just and equitable society for all. The journey towards gender parity is a long and complex one, but by learning from each other and working together, the U.S. and Europe can move closer to achieving this important goal.

ENVIRONMENTAL POLICY LESSONS

EUROPEAN APPROACHES
TO ENVIRONMENTAL CHALLENGES

European countries have long been at the forefront of addressing environmental challenges, implementing a variety of policy approaches that not only aim to combat climate change but also promote sustainable development. The European Union (EU) has established a comprehensive framework that integrates environmental considerations into all areas of policy-making. This approach reflects a commitment to the principle of sustainability, emphasizing long-term ecological health alongside economic and social goals. By prioritizing environmental standards, Europe has set a global example, showcasing how coordinated policy efforts can lead to meaningful change.

One notable aspect of European environmental policy is the emphasis on multilateralism and cooperation among nations. The EU has been instrumental in fostering collective action through agreements like the Paris Agreement, which seeks to limit global warming to well below two degrees Celsius. This collaborative spirit contrasts sharply with the often unilateral stance observed in U.S. environmental policy, which can be influenced by changing administrations. European nations tend to view environmental issues as shared responsibilities that require joint solutions, thereby enhancing their political leverage on the global stage.

The integration of environmental concerns into welfare state models also illustrates a distinctive European approach. Many European countries have successfully linked environmental policy to social welfare, recognizing that a healthy environment is essential for public well-being. For instance, initiatives promoting renewable energy not only address climate change but also create jobs and reduce energy poverty. This holistic view fosters a political environment where environmental sustainability is seen as a social imperative, reflecting a broader understanding of the interconnections between ecological health and societal welfare.

Furthermore, the impact of electoral systems on environmental policy cannot be overlooked. Many European countries employ proportional representation, which allows for a wider array of political parties, including those focused specifically on environmental issues, to gain seats in parliament. This system encourages diverse viewpoints and facilitates the incorporation of green policies into legislative agendas. In contrast, the majoritarian electoral system in the U.S. often sidelines smaller parties, limiting the breadth of political discourse on environmental challenges. The strength of green parties in Europe highlights the importance of political representation in advancing environmental agendas.

In summary, European approaches to environmental challenges provide valuable lessons for U.S. political discourse. The emphasis on multilateral cooperation, the integration of environmental and social policies, and the impact of electoral systems all contribute to a more cohesive and effective response to ecological issues. As global environmental challenges continue to mount, examining these European strategies can offer insights into how the U.S. might adopt more inclusive and effective policics that prioritize sustainable development. Bridging the divide between these differing political paradigms may well enhance the ability of both Europe and the U.S. to address pressing environmental concerns collaboratively.

Implications *for* US Political Discourse:
A TRANSATLANTIC PERSPECTIVE

The implications for US political discourse in light of European political practices are profound and multifaceted. Examining the successes and failures of European political systems offers valuable insights into alternative approaches to governance, social policy, and civic engagement that could potentially enrich and reshape the American political landscape. One of the most significant lessons that can be drawn from the European experience is the demonstrated effectiveness of welfare state models in promoting social equity and stability. The comparative analysis reveals that European nations tend to prioritize social welfare through comprehensive and often universal systems that offer robust healthcare, accessible education, and generous unemployment benefits. This stands in stark contrast to the more market-driven approach seen in the US, where social safety nets are often limited, fragmented, and reliant on individual responsibility. Understanding how these differing models influence political discourse can provide insights into how the US might address issues of inequality and social justice. By engaging with the arguments for and against robust social programs in Europe, the US can foster a more informed and inclusive political conversation about the role of government in ensuring the well-being of its citizens. This necessitates a deep dive into the economic consequences, societal impacts, and individual experiences associated with various welfare state models, moving beyond simplistic ideological pronouncements to evidence-based analysis.

Examining electoral systems further elucidates the divergence in political representation between the two regions. Many European countries utilize proportional representation (PR), or mixed-member proportional representation, which often leads to more diverse political parties and a wider range of viewpoints reflected in legislative bodies. PR systems allow smaller parties to gain representation based on their share of the overall vote, encouraging niche interests and minority groups to participate actively in the political process. This contrasts sharply with the US's winner-takes-all (single-member district) approach, which can marginalize smaller parties and reduce the overall diversity of political discourse. The dominance of the two-party system in the US often leads to tactical voting and strategic alliances that suppress alternative voices.

By analyzing the implications of these systems, US political actors may find avenues for reform that could enhance representation and encourage a more pluralistic dialogue among constituents. Ranked-choice voting, for example, offers a potential compromise that retains single-member districts while mitigating some of the drawbacks of the winner-takes-all system. Exploring these alternatives could potentially bridge the divide that has become so pronounced in recent years, fostering a political environment where a wider spectrum of perspectives is valued and incorporated into policymaking. Furthermore, studying the impact of PR systems on coalition governments in Europe can offer insights into how diverse political forces can work together to achieve common goals, even amidst ideological differences.

The role of political parties in shaping public policy is another area where lessons from Europe can inform US political discourse. In Europe, political parties often have a clearer ideological identity and exhibit greater cohesion, allowing for more decisive action on pressing issues, such as climate change, social justice, and economic inequality. Party platforms are typically more detailed and aligned with specific policy proposals, providing voters with clearly defined choices. This contrasts with the increasingly fragmented and polarized nature of US political parties, where ideological divisions can stymie effective governance and lead to gridlock. The influence of money and special interests in US politics further complicates the picture, often blurring party lines and hindering the pursuit of policies that serve the public good. By learning from European models of party organization and discipline, American political actors might develop strategies to foster greater internal collaboration and consensus-building. This could involve strengthening party leadership, promoting internal debate and dialogue, and developing mechanisms for enforcing party discipline on key votes. Ultimately, such efforts could lead to more effective policymaking and a greater sense of accountability to voters. Analyzing the role of party foundations and think tanks in shaping political discourse in Europe can also provide valuable lessons for the US, highlighting the importance of independent research and policy analysis in informing public debate.

Historical context plays a crucial role in shaping contemporary political ideologies across the Atlantic, influencing everything from party platforms to voter behavior. The legacy of colonialism, war, and economic development has left distinct marks on both European and American political landscapes. In Europe, the experience of two World Wars and the subsequent formation of the European Union have fostered a culture of multilateralism and cooperation, even amidst national differences. In contrast, the US has historically embraced a more isolationist and unilateral approach to foreign policy. Similarly, the lingering effects of colonialism continue to shape racial and ethnic relations in both regions, influencing political discourse and social policy. For instance, the rise of populism in both regions can be traced back to similar historical grievances and economic challenges, such as deindustrialization, globalization, and growing income inequality. However, the manifestations and responses differ significantly, reflecting distinct historical contexts and cultural norms. By examining these historical parallels and divergences, US political discourse can benefit from a deeper understanding of the roots of current ideological divides and populist movements. This deeper understanding can potentially lead to more effective engagement with disaffected voters, addressing their concerns in a nuanced and constructive manner, rather than resorting to divisive rhetoric and simplistic solutions. Exploring the historical narratives that underpin contemporary political ideologies can also help bridge cultural gaps and promote greater empathy and understanding across different segments of society.

Finally, the impact of political polarization in the US, as compared to European nations, reveals critical lessons about governance and civic engagement. While European countries also face challenges of polarization, the presence of supranational organizations like the

European Union can facilitate dialogue and compromise among member states. The EU provides a framework for addressing shared challenges, such as climate change, migration, and economic stability, fostering a sense of collective responsibility and encouraging collaboration across national borders. In contrast, the lack of similar structures in the US exacerbates tensions and hinders collaborative governance. The absence of a strong tradition of bipartisanship and the increasing reliance on partisan media outlets further contribute to the polarization of American politics. Embracing a more cooperative approach to politics, inspired by certain European practices, could help mitigate the detrimental effects of polarization in the US. This could involve promoting cross-party dialogue, encouraging civic education, and strengthening institutions that foster trust and cooperation. Furthermore, examining the role of civil society organizations and social movements in promoting social cohesion and bridging political divides in Europe can offer valuable insights for the US. Fostering a political culture that values dialogue, compromise, and evidence-based decision-making over division, conflict, and ideological dogma is essential for ensuring the long-term health and stability of American democracy. By learning from the successes and failures of European political systems, the US can embark on a path towards a more inclusive, equitable, and effective political discourse.

IMMIGRATION POLICIES AND POLITICAL RAMIFICATIONS

EUROPEAN IMMIGRATION POLICIES AND THEIR IMPACT

European immigration policies have evolved considerably over the decades, shaped by historical context, economic needs, and social dynamics. Unlike the more decentralized approach observed in the United States, European nations often implement policies under the framework of the European Union, which seeks to create a cohesive strategy for managing migration. The impact of these policies is multifaceted, affecting labor markets, social cohesion, and political landscapes across member states. The comparative nature of immigration policies in Europe versus the US reveals significant differences in how both regions perceive and handle the complexities of migration.

In Europe, immigration policies have increasingly been influenced by the need to address labor shortages, demographic changes, and humanitarian obligations. Countries like Germany and Sweden have adopted more inclusive approaches, welcoming refugees and skilled migrants to bolster their economies and address an aging population. Conversely, nations such as Hungary and Poland have pursued more restrictive policies, reflecting rising nationalism and concerns over cultural identity. This divergence highlights the role of political parties in shaping public opinion and legislative frameworks regarding immigration, often leading to polarized debates within and between countries.

The political ramifications of these immigration policies are profound. In many European countries, the rise of populist parties has been fueled by public dissatisfaction with immigration, leading to significant shifts in electoral outcomes. These parties often capitalize on fears associated with migration, advocating for stricter controls and fostering an "us versus them" narrative. This dynamic can destabilize traditional party systems and challenge the established political order, as seen in nations like Italy and France. The impact on governance becomes evident, as policymakers grapple with the dual demands of maintaining social cohesion while addressing the economic imperatives associated with migration.

Comparatively, the US immigration policy landscape is characterized by a more fragmented approach, with federal, state, and local governments often at odds over immigration enforcement and integration strategies. The political polarization surrounding immigration in the US has resulted in a contentious environment where bipartisan consensus remains elusive. This polarization not only affects legislative outcomes but also influences public discourse, creating a climate of divisiveness that complicates efforts to address immigration effectively. The comparison of European and US policies reveals how differing political contexts and electoral systems shape the discourse on immigration.

Ultimately, the lessons drawn from European immigration policies serve as a valuable resource for US policymakers grappling with similar challenges. By examining the various models employed across Europe, including integration strategies and the balance between humanitarian and economic considerations, the US can identify potential pathways for reform. In an era marked by increased global mobility and interconnectedness, understanding these transatlantic approaches offers critical insights into fostering more effective and humane immigration policies that reflect the values and needs of society as a whole.

US Immigration Policy:
HISTORICAL PERSPECTIVES

US immigration policy has evolved significantly over the centuries, influenced by a range of social, economic, and political factors. In the late 19th and early 20th centuries, waves of immigrants from Europe transformed the American landscape, prompting the establishment of more structured immigration laws. The Immigration Act of 1924, which imposed national quotas, marked a pivotal moment in US history. This legislation reflected prevailing attitudes of the time, favoring immigrants from Northern and Western Europe while severely restricting those from Southern and Eastern Europe. Such restrictions not only shaped the demographics of the United States but also laid the groundwork for ongoing debates regarding race, nationality, and the concept of the "American Dream."

The mid-20th century saw a shift in immigration policy, largely influenced by the civil rights movement and changing attitudes toward race and ethnicity. The Immigration and Nationality Act of 1965 abolished the quota system, allowing for a more diverse influx of immigrants. This policy change reflected broader societal values that emphasized equality and inclusion, marking a significant departure from earlier restrictive measures. The new law facilitated increased immigration from Asia, Latin America, and Africa, thereby reshaping the cultural fabric of the nation. The ramifications of this shift can still be observed today in the rich fabric of American society, where diverse cultural backgrounds contribute to a dynamic national identity.

The late 20th and early 21st centuries witnessed a resurgence of restrictive immigration policies, often driven by economic concerns and national security fears. The aftermath of the September 11 attacks in 2001 brought about heightened scrutiny of immigrants, particularly those from predominantly Muslim countries. The introduction of the Patriot

Act and subsequent legislation aimed at bolstering national security reflected a growing apprehension regarding immigration. This era highlighted the tension between the United States' foundational ideals of openness and its pragmatic responses to perceived threats. The political discourse surrounding immigration became increasingly polarized, with parties adopting starkly contrasting positions that continue to influence contemporary policy debates.

Throughout this historical trajectory, immigration policy has been a reflection of broader political ideologies and societal values. The role of political parties in shaping these policies cannot be overstated. Democrats have typically advocated for more inclusive and humanitarian approaches, emphasizing the contributions of immigrants to society. In contrast, Republican positions have often focused on national security and economic impacts, advocating for stricter regulations and enforcement. This divergence underscores the significance of political representation and the influence of electoral systems in shaping public policy across the Atlantic. The contrasting approaches to immigration in Europe and the US further illustrate how historical contexts and political paradigms inform contemporary debates.

As the United States grapples with its immigration policies today, the lessons drawn from Europe's varied approaches present valuable insights. European nations, with their own historical experiences of migration and integration, have developed different frameworks for addressing immigration challenges. The rise of populism on both sides of the Atlantic has also influenced immigration discourse, often framing it as a matter of national identity and sovereignty. By examining these historical perspectives, one can better understand the complexities of current immigration debates and the need for policies that not only reflect national interests but also honor the principles of inclusivity and diversity that have long defined the United States.

BRIDGING THE ATLANTIC
KEY TAKEAWAYS FROM
COMPARATIVE ANALYSIS

The comparative analysis of political systems in Europe and the United States reveals significant differences and similarities that shape governance and public policy. One of the primary takeaways is the contrasting welfare state models. European countries generally adopt a more extensive welfare state, characterized by higher taxation and a commitment to social safety nets. This approach not only aims to reduce inequality but also influences political ideology, encouraging parties to support broad social programs. In contrast, the US welfare model is more fragmented, promoting individual responsibility and market-driven solutions, which often leads to disparities in access to essential services such as healthcare and education.

Electoral systems play a crucial role in determining political representation across the Atlantic. European countries often employ proportional representation, which allows for a wider array of political parties to gain seats in parliament, reflecting diverse viewpoints. This system can lead to coalition governments that necessitate compromise and collaboration. Conversely, the US utilizes a winner-takes-all electoral framework, typically favoring two dominant parties. This structure can exacerbate polarization, as it discourages the presence of third parties and limits political diversity, impacting how policies are formulated and implemented.

The role of political parties in shaping public policy is also markedly different in Europe and the US. In Europe, political parties often have strong ideological foundations and cultivate a cohesive party identity, which can lead to more consistent policy agendas. In the US, political parties tend to be more fluid, with individual candidates frequently relying on personal branding that may diverge from established party ideologies. This divergence can complicate governance, as party loyalty can be overshadowed by individual political ambitions, resulting in challenges to effective policymaking.

Historical context further informs contemporary political ideologies in both regions. Europe's political landscape has been shaped by a history of social democracy and collective action, leading to a broader acceptance of state intervention in the economy. In contrast, the US's historical emphasis on individualism and limited government continues to influence its political culture, fostering resistance to expansive state involvement. These foundational beliefs manifest in current debates around issues such as healthcare, environmental policy, and social justice, illustrating how history shapes present governance.

Finally, examining contemporary political movements, such as populism, reveals transatlantic trends that demand attention. In both Europe and the US, populist movements have emerged as a response to perceived disenfranchisement, often leveraging anti-establishment sentiments. The rise of these movements highlights the impact of political polarization on governance, as they challenge traditional political institutions and ideologies. Understanding these dynamics through comparative analysis can provide valuable insights into addressing the challenges both regions face, particularly in areas like immigration policy, environmental strategies, and gender representation, ultimately fostering a more informed dialogue on bridging the divide across the Atlantic.

Future Directions *for* Transatlantic Relations

The future of transatlantic relations hinges on the ability of both Europe and the United States to navigate their respective political landscapes while recognizing shared interests and challenges. As political parties across the Atlantic evolve, understanding their role in shaping public policy becomes crucial. This involves a comparative analysis of how different electoral systems impact political representation. In Europe, proportional representation often leads to a broader spectrum of parties, while the winner-takes-all approach in the US can result in more polarized politics. By examining these systems, both regions can learn valuable lessons about inclusivity and the representation of diverse voices in governance.

Welfare state models present another vital area for future collaboration. European countries generally provide more extensive social safety nets, which can inform discussions in the US about healthcare, education, and social security reforms. As both regions grapple with aging populations and economic inequality, the exchange of ideas regarding welfare policies can lead to more robust solutions that benefit citizens on both sides of the Atlantic. This dialogue can enhance understanding of how different historical contexts have shaped contemporary ideologies, allowing for a richer appreciation of each other's political frameworks.

Populism has emerged as a significant force in both Europe and the US, often challenging traditional political structures. A transatlantic perspective on these movements reveals common grievances, such as economic disenfranchisement and cultural anxiety. However, the responses to populism differ widely, with European countries often adopting more centrist approaches to counteract extreme viewpoints, while the US political landscape has seen a more fragmented discourse. Future discussions should focus on identifying strategies that can mitigate the divisive effects of populism while fostering democratic resilience.

Environmental policy is another critical area where transatlantic relations can evolve. European approaches, which emphasize sustainability and ambitious climate goals, present an opportunity for the

US to rethink its environmental strategies. Collaborative efforts in technology transfer, renewable energy development, and regulatory frameworks can enhance both regions' capacities to address climate change. By learning from each other's successes and failures, Europe and the US can create a more unified front in the global fight against environmental degradation.

Finally, the role of supranational organizations in European politics offers lessons for US relations. Institutions such as the European Union exemplify how collective decision-making can enhance political stability and foster cooperation among diverse nations. As the US navigates its own political challenges, understanding how these organizations function and their implications for international relations can provide a roadmap for enhancing multilateral engagement. This engagement is essential for addressing global issues, from trade to security, and will ultimately shape the future of transatlantic relations, fostering a more interconnected and cooperative world.

COMPARATIVE ANALYSIS OF WELFARE STATE MODELS

Types *of* Welfare States *in* Europe

The welfare state is a fundamental aspect of European political systems, characterized by varying models that reflect historical, cultural, and economic contexts. Broadly, European welfare states can be categorized into three main types: the Nordic, the Continental, and the Anglo-Saxon model. Each of these models showcases distinct approaches to social security, health care, and public services, influencing political ideologies and party platforms across the continent. The Nordic model, known for its comprehensive welfare provisions, emphasizes universalism and high levels of public investment, aiming to reduce inequalities while promoting active labor market policies. In contrast, the Continental model, prevalent in countries like Germany and France, combines social insurance with a focus on maintaining social status, often leading to more fragmented access based on employment status.

The Anglo-Saxon model, represented by the United Kingdom and Ireland, tends to promote a more limited welfare state, focusing on means-tested benefits and a significant role for the private sector in delivering social services. This model reflects a more individualistic approach, where responsibilities are often shifted to the market and families. As a result, the welfare provisions in these countries are less comprehensive than their Nordic counterparts, leading to ongoing debates about the adequacy and accessibility of social safety nets. The differences among these models highlight the complexity of political discussions surrounding welfare in Europe, where parties often align their platforms based on these foundational principles.

Electoral systems across Europe also play a crucial role in shaping welfare policies and political representation. Many European countries utilize proportional representation, which allows for a broader spectrum of political parties to gain seats in parliament. This system encourages coalition governments, often resulting in compromises that reflect diverse social interests and facilitate the expansion of welfare programs. In contrast, the United States employs a majoritarian electoral system that tends to favor two dominant parties, limiting the scope of welfare discourse and often restricting significant reforms. The comparative analysis of these electoral systems underscores how political representation directly influences policy outcomes, particularly in the realm of social welfare.

The historical context of each European welfare model is also vital in understanding contemporary political ideologies. Post-World War

II reconstruction and the rise of social democracy in many countries led to the establishment of robust welfare systems aimed at preventing the social upheavals experienced during the interwar period. The legacies of these historical events continue to shape public attitudes toward government intervention and the social contract. Political parties in Europe, often rooted in these historical narratives, leverage them to advocate for welfare policies that align with their ideological foundations, demonstrating the interplay between history and contemporary governance.

Lastly, the rise of populism across Europe has prompted a reevaluation of welfare policies, as parties on both the left and right respond to changing public sentiments. Populist movements often critique existing welfare systems, arguing that they do not serve the interests of the "ordinary people." This discourse has significant implications for political parties, as they navigate the challenge of addressing legitimate concerns about immigration, economic inequality, and social cohesion while maintaining commitment to welfare principles. The lessons learned from Europe's diverse welfare state models underscore the importance of adapting policies to meet evolving societal needs, offering valuable insights for the political landscape in the United States as it grapples with similar challenges.

The U.S Welfare System: Challenges *and* Opportunities

The US welfare system has long been a subject of debate, characterized by both significant challenges and notable opportunities. In contrast to the more expansive welfare models found in many European countries, the US system is often seen as fragmented and limited in scope. This discrepancy raises important questions about the effectiveness of welfare programs in addressing poverty and inequality. The challenges inherent in the US welfare system include bureaucratic inefficiencies, stigmatization of recipients, and inadequacies in coverage for vulnerable populations. While many European nations have developed comprehensive safety nets that prioritize social solidarity, the US approach has traditionally emphasized individual responsibility, which can leave many without adequate support.

One of the primary challenges in the US welfare system is its reliance on means-tested programs that can create disincentives for recipients to seek employment. Programs such as Temporary Assistance for Needy Families (TANF) provide crucial support, yet the stringent eligibility requirements and time limits can lead to cycles of poverty rather than pathways out of it. In contrast, many European welfare states offer more universal benefits that allow for greater mobility and security among their citizens. This comparative view highlights the potential for the US to reevaluate its approach to welfare, potentially looking towards European models that emphasize inclusivity and support for all citizens, rather than only those who meet specific criteria.

Despite these challenges, there are opportunities for reform within the US welfare system that could enhance its effectiveness. The rising awareness of income inequality and the increasing influence of social movements advocating for worker rights provide a fertile ground for change. Additionally, the ongoing discussions surrounding healthcare reform, particularly in the wake of the COVID-19 pandemic, signal a growing recognition of the need for a more cohesive approach to social welfare. By examining successful elements of European welfare models, US policymakers can identify strategies that promote social equity while also fostering economic growth.

The role of political parties in shaping the welfare debate is also critical. In the US, the political landscape is often polarized, with the Democratic Party generally advocating for increased welfare provisions while the Republican Party tends to prioritize reducing government spending and promoting individualism. This division complicates the development of a unified welfare strategy and often results in piecemeal solutions rather than comprehensive policy reform. In contrast, many European political parties, regardless of their ideological leanings, recognize the importance of a robust welfare state and are more likely to collaborate on reforms that enhance social welfare.

In conclusion, the US welfare system embodies a complex interplay of challenges and opportunities that warrant serious consideration. By learning from the European experience, the US can explore pathways that strengthen its social safety net while addressing the needs of its most vulnerable citizens. The potential for reform is significant, particularly as public attitudes shift and political movements gain momentum. Bridging the divide between these two political paradigms not only offers lessons for welfare reform but also highlights the importance of cooperation and dialogue in achieving a more equitable society.

POLITICAL LESSONS FROM EUROPE AND THE U.S

INTRODUCTION TO TRANSATLANTIC POLITICAL DYNAMICS

Overview *of* European *and* US Political Landscapes

The political landscapes of Europe and the United States present a complex interplay of historical context, cultural values, and institutional frameworks that shape their governance and public policy. At the core of this comparison lies the welfare state model, which varies significantly between the two regions. European countries tend to embrace a more comprehensive welfare system that prioritizes social safety nets and universal healthcare, while the US model is characterized by a more market-oriented approach with limited government involvement in providing social services. This divergence in welfare policies informs broader discussions about economic equity, social justice, and the role of government in citizens' lives, highlighting the advantages and challenges inherent in each system.

Electoral systems also play a crucial role in shaping political representation on both sides of the Atlantic. In Europe, many countries utilize proportional representation, allowing for a wider array of political parties to gain seats in legislative bodies. This system encourages coalition governments and often results in more diverse viewpoints being represented in policy discussions. Conversely, the US employs a first-past-the-post electoral system, which often leads to a two-party dominance, limiting the political spectrum and stifling third-party emergence. The implications of these differing electoral frameworks extend beyond representation; they influence voter engagement, political polarization, and the overall health of democratic practices.

Political parties are pivotal in both European and US contexts, acting as conduits for public policy formation and representation of various interest groups. In Europe, political parties often align closely with ideological movements, resulting in well-defined party platforms that reflect the nuances of voters' preferences. This contrasts with the US, where parties may exhibit broader ideologies that can sometimes obscure distinct policy positions. The role of parties in shaping public discourse, mobilizing voters, and influencing legislation is significant in both regions, yet the effectiveness and accountability of these parties vary greatly due to their structural differences and the political culture that surrounds them.

The historical context of each region has left a lasting impact on contemporary political ideologies. In Europe, the aftermath of World War II and the subsequent Cold War shaped a collective commitment to social democracy and human rights, fostering an environment that values community welfare. In contrast, the US political ideology has been heavily influenced by individualism and capitalism, promoting a belief in limited government and personal responsibility. These underlying principles continue to influence contemporary debates on issues such as immigration, environmental policy, and gender representation, revealing the deep-seated values that drive political decisions in each region.

The rise of populism is another critical element in the transatlantic political dialogue, reflecting broader discontent with traditional political institutions. Both Europe and the US have witnessed the emergence of populist movements that challenge established parties, often leveraging economic anxiety and cultural grievances. These movements highlight the growing divide in political ideologies and the need for a nuanced understanding of public sentiment. As the political landscapes evolve, examining the lessons learned from each region can provide valuable insights for bridging divides and fostering collaborative approaches to global challenges, including environmental policies and governance strategies that address the needs of diverse populations.

Historical Context *of* Transatlantic Relations

The historical context of transatlantic relations is essential for understanding the intricacies of contemporary political dynamics between Europe and the United States. The roots of these relations can be traced back to the colonial period when European powers, particularly Britain, established settlements in the New World. This initial connection laid the groundwork for a complex interplay of cultural, political, and economic exchanges that would evolve over centuries. The American Revolution marked a pivotal moment, as it not only severed colonial ties but also inspired revolutionary movements in Europe, highlighting a shared value in democratic ideals and self-governance. The echoes of the American Revolution resonated across the Atlantic, fueling

Enlightenment ideals and contributing to the ferment that would ultimately lead to the French Revolution. This period established a transatlantic dialogue on liberty, equality, and the rights of man, even as the specific interpretations and implementations of these ideals diverged on either side of the ocean.

The 19th and early 20th centuries witnessed significant developments that shaped transatlantic relations, including industrialization, immigration, and the rise of national identities. The waves of European immigrants to the United States contributed to the country's demographic and cultural diversity, acting as both a bridge and a potential source of tension. These immigrants brought with them not only their labor but also their languages, customs, and political beliefs, influencing the American cultural mosaic and, in turn, maintaining ties with their homelands. Simultaneously, the industrial revolution spurred economic competition and collaboration between European powers and the United States. Political ideologies began to take shape in response to these changes, with the emergence of socialism, liberalism, and various nationalist movements in Europe, contrasted by the American experience of frontier individualism and capitalist expansion. These differing political paradigms influenced the evolution of political parties and their platforms on both sides of the Atlantic, as well as fostering debates over the role of the state in regulating the economy and providing social welfare. The rise of imperialism further complicated transatlantic relations, as European powers sought to expand their colonial empires, often leading to clashes with American interests and ideals, particularly in regions like Latin America.

The aftermath of World War II marked another critical juncture in transatlantic relations, as the United States and Western European nations sought to rebuild and stabilize their economies. With much of Europe devastated, the United States emerged as a global superpower, wielding significant economic and political influence. Institutions such as the Marshall Plan, designed to provide massive economic aid to war-torn Europe, and NATO, a military alliance aimed at deterring Soviet aggression, symbolized a commitment to collective security and economic cooperation. The establishment of these institutions not only solidified the transatlantic partnership but also shaped the geopolitical landscape for decades to come. Moreover, the establishment of welfare state models in various European countries offered a contrasting approach to social policy compared to the United States. This divergence in welfare state frameworks would later become a significant point of comparison, influencing public policy debates and political discourse on both sides. The Cold War further cemented the transatlantic alliance, as the shared threat of Soviet communism united Western Europe and the United States in a common cause.

The late 20th century and early 21st century brought new challenges and transformations, including the rise of populism, globalization, and political polarization. The collapse of the Soviet Union and the end of the Cold War led to a reevaluation of the transatlantic relationship, as new threats and opportunities emerged. Globalization, with its increased interconnectedness and economic interdependence, presented both benefits and challenges, leading to debates over trade, labor standards, and environmental regulations. Populist movements gained traction in both Europe and the United States, often fueled by economic anxieties, cultural grievances, and disillusionment with traditional political parties. These movements have reshaped electoral systems and political representation, raising questions about governance and the role of political parties in addressing public concerns. The 2008 financial crisis exposed vulnerabilities in the global economic system and further fueled populist sentiments. The contrasting approaches to immigration and environmental policy further illustrate how historical context continues to influence contemporary political ideologies and debates across the Atlantic. For instance, European nations, grappling with aging populations and labor shortages, have often adopted more liberal immigration policies than the United States, while also taking a more proactive approach to addressing climate change.

Furthermore, the rise of supranational organizations like the European Union has profoundly impacted transatlantic relations. The EU has emerged as a significant economic and political power, capable of negotiating with the United States on a range of issues, from trade to security. However, the EU's integration process has also faced challenges, including Brexit and the rise of nationalist sentiments within member states, creating new complexities for the transatlantic partnership. Debates over sovereignty, national identity, and the role of supranational institutions continue to shape political discourse on both sides of the Atlantic. The election of Donald Trump in the United States further strained transatlantic relations, as his "America First" policy challenged the traditional norms of international cooperation and multilateralism. His administration's withdrawal from the Paris Agreement on climate change and the Iran nuclear deal, as well as his criticism of NATO allies, created deep divisions within the transatlantic community.

In summary, the historical context of transatlantic relations reveals the complex interplay of cultural, political, and economic factors that have shaped the political landscape on both sides. Understanding these historical developments is crucial for examining how contemporary issues, such as gender representation, political polarization, and the influence of supranational organizations, are framed within a transatlantic perspective. Gender representation in politics, for example, has followed different trajectories in Europe and the United States, influenced by varying cultural norms and political traditions. Similarly, political polarization, while a growing concern on both sides of the Atlantic, manifests itself in different ways, reflecting distinct historical and social contexts. By analyzing these dynamics, we can identify lessons that inform future collaboration and dialogue between Europe and the United States in addressing shared challenges and opportunities. Moving forward, a nuanced understanding of the historical context of transatlantic relations is essential for navigating the complexities of the 21st century and ensuring a strong and resilient partnership between Europe and the United States. This partnership will be crucial in addressing global challenges such as climate change, economic inequality, and the rise of authoritarianism, requiring a sustained commitment to dialogue, cooperation, and mutual understanding.

POLITICAL ADVANTAGES IN EUROPE vs. THE US

Social Welfare Models:
A COMPARATIVE APPROACH

Social welfare models serve as a crucial lens through which to understand the political landscapes of Europe and the United States, revealing the divergent philosophies and practices that shape public policy. In Europe, the welfare state is often characterized by a commitment to universalism, where social safety nets are designed to provide broad protection for all citizens, reflecting a collective responsibility for individual well-being. This model is underpinned by the belief that access to healthcare, education, and social security is a fundamental right, which has fostered a comprehensive approach to social welfare across various European nations. In contrast, the United States predominantly adheres to a more fragmented welfare system, emphasizing individual responsibility and market solutions, which has resulted in significant gaps in coverage and access for vulnerable populations.

The comparative analysis of welfare state models highlights not only the differences in policy outcomes but also the influence of historical context on contemporary political ideologies. European welfare states have evolved from a history of collectivism, shaped by post-World War II reconstruction and a strong labor movement, which emphasized social solidarity and class compromise. In the U.S., the welfare system emerged from a tradition of liberalism and individualism, influenced by a distinct set of historical events such as the Great Depression and civil rights movements. These historical trajectories have shaped how political parties in both regions approach issues of social welfare, with European parties generally advocating for more expansive welfare policies compared to the more conservative stances often seen in American politics.

Electoral systems play a pivotal role in determining political representation, which subsequently impacts the formulation of welfare policies. In Europe, proportional representation systems often lead to multi-party environments, allowing for a broader spectrum of political views, including those favoring stronger welfare measures. This inclusivity can promote coalition-building, resulting in policies that reflect a wider array of societal needs. Conversely, the U.S. employs a winner-takes-all electoral system that tends to favor the two-party structure, often sidelining alternative voices and limiting the political discourse surrounding social welfare. This dynamic can lead to more polarized debates and hinder comprehensive reforms that could address the needs of underrepresented groups.

Political parties in both regions play a critical role in shaping public policy, with their platforms often reflecting the prevailing social welfare philosophies. In Europe, social democratic and green parties frequently advocate for robust welfare protections, environmental sustainability, and progressive social policies, leading to a more expansive interpretation of the welfare state. In contrast, American political parties, particularly the Republican Party, have historically sought to limit the scope of government involvement in welfare, promoting a narrative of personal responsibility and economic freedom. This divergence shapes not only the welfare policies enacted but also the public's perception of the role of government in individuals' lives, further influencing electoral outcomes and party strategies.

Finally, the rise of populism in both Europe and the U.S. presents a significant challenge to traditional welfare models, as these movements often capitalize on economic grievances and feelings of disenfranchisement. Populist parties tend to promote anti-establishment sentiments, which can undermine established welfare systems by questioning the legitimacy of existing social contracts. This phenomenon necessitates a reevaluation of how political parties engage with the electorate on welfare issues, as well as an examination of the potential for transatlantic lessons in addressing common challenges. By analyzing these dynamics, we can better understand the implications for governance and social policy in both regions, ultimately bridging the divide in political discourse across the Atlantic.

Governance Structures *and* Political Stability

Governance structures are fundamental to understanding the political stability of nations, particularly when comparing the frameworks of Europe and the United States. In Europe, political stability often hinges on a mix of parliamentary systems and proportional representation, which fosters a multiparty environment. This contrasts sharply with the predominantly two-party system in the United States, where the winner-takes-all approach can lead to significant polarization. The European model allows for coalition governments, which may enhance political stability by requiring collaboration among diverse parties, thereby reflecting a broader range of public opinions. Such systems can mitigate the extremes of political discourse, creating an environment where compromise is not only necessary but expected.

The historical context of governance structures reveals important lessons about political stability. In many European countries, the legacy of post-World War II reconstruction led to the establishment of welfare states and social contracts designed to promote stability and economic security. These models foster a sense of collective responsibility and engagement, enabling citizens to feel invested in the political process. Conversely, the US governance model, rooted in a strong emphasis on individualism, often results in a more competitive political landscape. This divergence in foundational ideologies influences contemporary political behavior and public policy outcomes, with European nations tending to prioritize social welfare and equity more than their American counterparts.

The impact of electoral systems on political representation further illustrates differences in governance structures. Proportional representation in Europe allows for a more accurate reflection of the electorate's preferences, often resulting in a diverse array of parties in parliament. This diversity can strengthen democracy by ensuring minority voices are heard, although it may also lead to fragmented legislatures and complex coalition negotiations. In contrast, the US system often marginalizes third-party candidates and minimizes the representation of minority viewpoints, which can exacerbate feelings of disenfranchisement among certain voter blocs. Understanding these electoral dynamics is crucial for comprehending how political stability is maintained or challenged across the Atlantic.

Political parties play a pivotal role in shaping public policy, with their structures and strategies reflecting the broader governance frameworks. In Europe, political parties often align along ideological lines, promoting comprehensive platforms on issues such as environmental policy, immigration, and social justice. This alignment fosters coherent policy-making and allows parties to present clear alternatives to the electorate. In the United States, however, the dominance of the two-party system can lead to more transactional politics, where party affiliation often supersedes substantive policy debates. This difference impacts not only governance but also the electorate's engagement with political processes, influencing public trust and participation rates.

Lastly, the influence of populism highlights the vulnerabilities within both governance structures. In Europe, rising populist movements have capitalized on economic discontent and a perception of disconnection from traditional political elites. These movements challenge established parties and can disrupt the political landscape, posing questions about the resilience of democratic institutions. In the US, populism has similarly emerged, often intensifying political polarization and straining governance. The transatlantic perspective on these movements reveals that while the roots of populism may vary, the underlying issues of economic inequality, cultural displacement, and political alienation resonate across both continents. By examining these dynamics, we can better understand the intricate relationship between governance structures and political stability in a rapidly changing global landscape.

LESSONS FROM DIFFERENT POLITICAL PARADIGMS

Understanding *the* European Social Model

The European Social Model (ESM) represents a distinctive approach to governance and welfare that emphasizes social equity, collective responsibility, and the provision of universal services. Rooted in historical developments following World War II, the ESM emerged as a response to the need for social cohesion and economic stability in a rapidly changing world. It prioritizes the protection of citizens' rights and welfare while promoting economic competitiveness. This model contrasts sharply with the United States' more individualistic and market-driven approach, highlighting significant differences in political ideologies and the role of government in society. Understanding these differences is crucial for analyzing the broader political landscape across the Atlantic.

At the core of the ESM is the commitment to a comprehensive welfare state that ensures access to healthcare, education, and social services for all citizens. This commitment reflects a consensus among European countries that social protection is a fundamental right, not merely a market commodity. In comparison, the United States has historically favored a mixed approach that combines private and public welfare initiatives, often leading to gaps in coverage and disparities in access to essential services. This divergence illustrates how the underlying values of political parties in each region shape their respective approaches to public policy, with European parties generally advocating for more robust social safety nets.

Electoral systems in Europe differ markedly from those in the United States, influencing political representation and party dynamics. Many European countries employ proportional representation, allowing for a broader spectrum of political parties to gain representation in legislatures. This system fosters coalition governments and encourages collaboration across party lines, reflecting a more consensus-driven approach to policymaking. In contrast, the US utilizes a winner-takes-all system that often marginalizes smaller parties and leads to increased polarization. Understanding these electoral mechanisms is vital for grasping how political parties in both regions navigate the complexities of governance and public policy formulation.

The historical context of European countries also plays a significant role in shaping contemporary political ideologies. The legacy of social democracy, labor movements, and post-war reconstruction has led to a collective understanding of the state's responsibility towards its citizens. In contrast, the US political landscape has been shaped by ideals of rugged individualism and limited government intervention, resulting in a different set of challenges in addressing social issues. This historical perspective is essential for examining current political movements, including populism, which have gained traction on both sides of the Atlantic as a reaction to perceived failures of established political structures.

In addressing contemporary challenges such as climate change, gender representation, and immigration, European approaches often offer valuable lessons for US political discourse. European countries have made significant strides in implementing progressive environmental policies, highlighting the role of government in leading sustainable initiatives. Similarly, the emphasis on gender parity in political representation serves as a model for enhancing diversity in governance. By analyzing these aspects within the framework of the ESM, one can better appreciate the potential for transatlantic dialogue and cooperation. Bridging the divide between these political paradigms may not only enrich the understanding of each region's approach but also foster collaborative solutions to shared global challenges.

The American Liberal Democracy

The American liberal democracy stands as a distinctive political model, a testament to both the enduring allure of individual freedom and the inherent complexities of governing a diverse populace. Rooted deeply in the fertile intellectual ground of the Enlightenment, it champions the primacy of civil liberties, the impartial rule of law, and a meticulously crafted system of checks and balances designed to prevent the concentration of power. This framework, meticulously laid out by the Founding Fathers, has not only indelibly shaped the American political landscape but has also served as an inspiration, albeit often a contested one, for democratic movements across the globe. However, to fully grasp the nuances of the American experiment, its unique characteristics must be examined in juxtaposition with the political paradigms prevalent in Europe, where social democracy, with its emphasis on more extensive welfare provisions and collective decision-making processes, often presents a contrasting vision of liberal governance.

One of the most readily apparent and consequential differences between the American and European political systems lies in their respective electoral frameworks. The United States, steeped in its historical distrust of centralized power and its emphasis on local representation, employs a predominantly first-past-the-post (FPTP) electoral system. In this system, the candidate who receives the most votes in a given district wins, regardless of whether they secure an absolute majority. While proponents argue that this system promotes stable majority governments and clear accountability, it has also been criticized for fostering a two-party system, disenfranchising smaller parties, and leading to significant disparities in political representation. The "winner-takes-all" nature of FPTP can effectively silence minority voices and exacerbate political polarization. Conversely, many European countries, recognizing the value of wider representation, utilize proportional representation (PR) systems. In PR systems, the number of seats a party wins in the legislature is directly proportional to the percentage of votes it receives. This allows for a broader spectrum of political parties and ideologies to gain representation, fostering a more diverse and inclusive political landscape. The presence of smaller parties in the legislature can lead to more nuanced debates, greater responsiveness to niche issues, and ultimately, a more representative government. This fundamental divergence in electoral systems has profound implications for political representation, influencing not only the extent to which diverse voices are heard, but also the ability of smaller parties to influence the direction of public policy and hold larger parties accountable.

Political parties, the engines of modern democracy, play a crucial role in shaping public policy in both the US and Europe, yet their functions, structures, and overall influence differ markedly. In the United States, the Democratic and Republican parties dominate the political landscape, creating a duopoly that often leads to intense polarization and legislative gridlock. While both parties encompass a broad range of ideologies, the increasing emphasis on partisan loyalty and the rise of ideological purity tests within each party have made compromise increasingly difficult. The result is often a political system paralyzed by partisan bickering, unable to effectively address pressing national challenges. In contrast, European political parties frequently operate within multiparty coalitions, a necessity dictated by the prevalence of proportional representation. This collaborative environment necessitates constant negotiation and compromise, fostering a political culture that prioritizes consensus-building over ideological intransigence. While coalition governments can be less stable than single-party governments, they often lead to more progressive policy outcomes, particularly in areas such as social welfare, environmental regulation, and economic equality, where collective action and broad-based support are essential for addressing complex challenges. The need to forge consensus forces parties to engage in dialogue, consider diverse perspectives, and ultimately, craft policies that reflect the needs and priorities of a wider segment of the population.

Delving deeper into the transatlantic divide, the historical context of each region significantly influences contemporary political ideologies and policy preferences. In Europe, the collective trauma of World War II and the subsequent rise of social democratic movements led to the establishment of robust welfare states. The horrors of the war underscored the importance of social solidarity and the need for a strong social safety net to protect vulnerable populations from economic hardship and social exclusion. This historical experience engendered a political culture that values social equity, collective responsibility, and the active role of government in ensuring the well-being of its citizens. Meanwhile, American political ideology is deeply rooted in individualism, a historical suspicion of government intervention, and a strong belief in the power of free markets. The American narrative of self-reliance and entrepreneurialism often clashes with the European emphasis on collective responsibility and social welfare. This fundamental divergence in values has profound implications for how each region approaches pressing issues such as immigration, gender representation, and the rise of populism. European nations, often drawing upon their historical experience with multiculturalism and social inclusivity, tend to adopt more inclusive policies towards immigrants and refugees, while the US grapples with increasing polarization and nativist sentiments. Similarly, European countries have made significant strides in promoting gender equality and women's representation in politics, while the US continues to lag behind in this area.

Finally, the transatlantic relationship, a cornerstone of global politics and economics, is increasingly shaped by the rise of supranational organizations in Europe, most notably the European Union (EU). The EU, a complex and evolving entity, facilitates cooperation among member states on a wide range of issues, including trade, security, environmental policy, and immigration. The EU's economic and political policies have a significant impact not only on Europe but also on the global economy and international relations, resonating across the Atlantic and influencing the policies of the United States. The EU's regulatory framework, particularly in areas such as environmental protection and data privacy, often sets global standards that American companies must adhere to in order to compete in the European market. This interconnectedness highlights the importance of understanding the lessons that can be drawn from European approaches to governance, particularly in areas where the US faces significant challenges. For example, the EU's commitment to renewable energy and its efforts to combat climate change offer valuable insights for American policymakers seeking to address the urgent threat of global warming. Similarly, the EU's robust social safety net and its commitment to economic equality provide a model for addressing income inequality and poverty in the United States. By examining these intricate differences and similarities, one can better appreciate the nuanced landscape of political ideologies and practices that define liberal democracy on both sides of the Atlantic, fostering a more informed and constructive dialogue about the future of democracy in a rapidly changing world. This transatlantic dialogue is essential for ensuring that liberal democracies remain resilient and capable of addressing the challenges of the 21st century, from climate change and economic inequality to the rise of authoritarianism and the spread of misinformation.

ANALYZING POLITICAL PARTIES ACROSS THE ATLANTIC

The Role *of* Political Parties *in* Europe

The role of political parties in Europe is multifaceted and significantly shapes the continent's political landscape, distinguishing it from other regions, most notably the United States. Unlike the United States, where a dominant two-party system often prevails, many European countries operate within multiparty systems. This diversity enables a broader representation of viewpoints, fostering a more nuanced political discourse and facilitating the formation of coalitions that can lead to more comprehensive and broadly supported public policies. Political parties in Europe often align themselves with specific ideological frameworks, such as social democracy, liberalism, conservatism, green politics, or even regionalist agendas, allowing for a rich variations of political discourse that reflects the varied interests and values of the populace. This spectrum of ideologies contributes to a vibrant and often contentious political environment where compromise and coalition-building are essential skills for effective governance.

European political parties also play a critical role in shaping public policy by acting as vital intermediaries between citizens and the government. They articulate the interests and concerns of their constituents, translating them into concrete legislative agendas and advocating for their implementation. This process is often perceived as more transparent and participatory than in the U.S., where political parties can sometimes be criticized as more hierarchical and centralized, with power concentrated in the hands of party elites. In Europe, grassroots movements within parties frequently influence policy direction, leading to a dynamic interplay between party leadership and membership that encourages responsiveness to public sentiment. This bottom-up approach helps to ensure that party platforms reflect the evolving needs and priorities of the electorate, fostering a sense of ownership and engagement in the political process. Furthermore, European parties are heavily involved in voter mobilization, education, and outreach, striving to inform citizens and encourage active participation in elections and other forms of political engagement.

Furthermore, the unique historical context of Europe has profoundly influenced contemporary political ideologies and party dynamics. The devastating legacy of World War II, the ideological divisions of the Cold War, and the subsequent process of European integration have fostered a unique political environment characterized by a strong commitment to multilateralism, social welfare, and the rule of law. Political parties in Europe often prioritize collective values and social justice, reflecting a deep-seated historical understanding of the need for solidarity and cooperation in the face of past divisions and conflicts. This contrasts sharply with the U.S. political landscape, where individualism, market-oriented policies, and a more skeptical view of government intervention are often more prevalent. The European emphasis on social cohesion and equality has led to the development of extensive welfare states and robust social safety nets, policies often championed by social democratic and left-leaning parties.

Electoral systems in Europe also significantly contribute to the effectiveness of political parties in representing diverse interests and ensuring a more inclusive political process. Proportional representation, which is common in many European nations, encourages smaller parties to gain seats in parliament, ensuring that minority views and specialized interests are included in the political dialogue. This system fosters a more pluralistic political environment, where a wider range of voices are heard and considered in the policymaking process. This stands in stark contrast to the U.S.'s winner-takes-all approach, which can marginalize smaller parties and limit political diversity, often leading to a situation where the concerns of significant portions of the population are not adequately addressed. The implications of these differing electoral systems are profound, as they influence not only party formation and representation but also voter engagement, satisfaction with the political process, and the overall legitimacy of government. Proportional representation often leads to higher voter turnout and a greater sense of political efficacy among citizens.

Lastly, the rise of populism, nationalism, and Euroscepticism in both Europe and the U.S. highlights the significant challenges faced by traditional political parties in an increasingly complex and interconnected world. In Europe, populist movements have emerged in response to a variety of factors, including economic crises, immigration, growing inequality, and widespread dissatisfaction with the political establishment and perceived democratic deficits within the European

Union. These movements often capitalize on public discontent, exploiting anxieties about national identity, cultural change, and economic insecurity, and challenging the status quo by advocating for radical policy changes and a rejection of established political norms. This has prompted established parties to reassess their strategies and policies, forcing them to address the underlying causes of public discontent and to find new ways to connect with voters who feel alienated and disenfranchised. The transatlantic perspective on these developments underscores the necessity for political parties to adapt and evolve in response to changing voter sentiments, effectively communicate their values and policy proposals, and demonstrate their ability to address the complex challenges facing their societies, ensuring they remain relevant and responsive in an increasingly polarized and uncertain political environment. Furthermore, the rise of new technologies and social media platforms has significantly altered the landscape of political communication, requiring parties to adapt their strategies to effectively engage with voters online and combat the spread of misinformation and disinformation.

The Role *of* Political Parties *in the* US

Political parties in the United States serve as essential vehicles for political organization, representation, and policy-making. Unlike many European countries, where multi-party systems often dominate, the U.S. operates primarily under a two-party system, consisting of the Democratic and Republican parties. This structure significantly shapes the political landscape, influencing electoral outcomes and governance. Political parties in the U.S. not only mobilize voters but also provide a framework for political discourse, shaping the ideological contours of public policy. The mechanisms of party operation and their interaction with the electoral system highlight the unique dynamics at play in American politics.

The historical context of political parties in the U.S. reveals a trajectory marked by evolution and adaptation. Originating from the early factions in the late 18th century, with figures like Alexander Hamilton and Thomas Jefferson representing nascent Federalist and Anti-Federalist ideologies, American political parties have transformed in response to changing societal needs and pressures. The initial debates centered on the balance of power between the federal government and the states, economic policy, and foreign relations. Over time, the party system underwent several realignments, reflecting major shifts in the electorate's priorities. The demise of the Federalist Party, the rise and fall of the Whig Party, and the emergence of the Republican Party in the mid-19th century around the issue of slavery demonstrate this fluidity. The emergence of key issues, such as civil rights, economic policy, and healthcare, has driven the parties to redefine their platforms and alignments. The New Deal era, for example, saw a dramatic shift in the Democratic Party's platform towards a more interventionist role for the government in the economy, attracting new constituencies and solidifying its base for decades. This process of realignment has often reflected the broader societal shifts, paralleling changes in demographics, economic conditions, and cultural attitudes. Understanding this historical evolution is crucial for grasping how contemporary political ideologies are formed and contested within the U.S. political framework. The legacy of past struggles and compromises continues to shape the political discourse and inform the strategies of modern-day parties.

In contrast to European political parties, which frequently engage with a wider spectrum of ideological positions due to their multi-party systems, U.S. parties tend to be more polarized. This polarization has profound implications for governance and policy-making, often resulting in gridlock and a lack of bipartisan cooperation. The causes of this polarization are multifaceted, ranging from the rise of partisan media outlets that reinforce existing biases to the increasing sorting of voters along ideological lines. Gerrymandering, the practice of drawing electoral district boundaries to favor one party over another, also contributes to the problem by creating safe seats for incumbents and reducing the incentive for compromise. The rigid party lines can stifle compromise, making it challenging to address pressing issues such as climate change, healthcare reform, and immigration. For example, attempts to pass comprehensive immigration reform have repeatedly failed due to deep divisions between the parties on issues such as border security, pathways to citizenship, and the treatment of undocumented immigrants. This phenomenon raises questions about the efficacy of the American political system in responding to complex challenges, especially when compared to the more consensus-driven approaches observed in many European democracies. In countries like Germany or the Netherlands, coalition governments are common, requiring parties to negotiate and compromise to form a governing majority.

Political parties in the U.S. also play a vital role in shaping public policy through their influence on legislative agendas and governance. The party in power typically sets the tone for policy initiatives, reflecting its ideological commitments and priorities. For instance, during periods of Republican control, there is often a focus on tax cuts, deregulation, and conservative judicial appointments, while Democratic administrations tend to prioritize social programs, environmental protection, and progressive tax policies. This process is further complicated by the checks and balances inherent in the U.S. political system, where executive, legislative, and judicial branches interact. The President, as the leader of their party, can use their executive powers to advance their agenda, but their success depends on their ability to work with Congress, which is often divided along party lines. The judiciary, particularly the Supreme Court, also plays a crucial role in shaping public policy by interpreting laws and determining their constitutionality. The dominance of political parties in framing policy debates can lead to significant variances in public policy outcomes between administrations, demonstrating the power wielded by party organizations in shaping the direction of national discourse. The Affordable Care Act (ACA), passed under the Obama administration, and subsequent attempts by Republicans to repeal it, exemplify this dynamic, highlighting how party control can lead to dramatic shifts in healthcare policy.

Beyond their influence on legislative and executive branches, political parties also exert considerable influence on the judicial branch through the appointment process. Presidents typically nominate judges who align with their party's ideological leanings, leading to increasingly polarized judicial confirmations and debates over the role of the courts in shaping public policy. This politicization of the judiciary has significant implications for the interpretation of laws and the protection of individual rights, further reinforcing the power of political parties in American society.

Examining the role of political parties across the Atlantic underscores critical lessons for both American and European political landscapes. The contrasting party systems reveal different approaches to representation and governance, highlighting the advantages and challenges inherent in each model. The U.S. two-party system, while providing stability and clear lines of accountability, can also lead to political gridlock and the marginalization of minority viewpoints. In contrast, European multi-party systems, while offering greater representation and more diverse policy options, can be less stable and more prone to coalition breakdowns. By analyzing these differences, political actors and citizens can glean insights into enhancing democratic practices, fostering political engagement, and ultimately bridging the divides that characterize contemporary political life. For example, the U.S. could learn from European models of campaign finance reform to reduce the influence of money in politics, while European countries could study American strategies for mobilizing voters and increasing political participation. The comparative analysis of political parties not only enriches our understanding of their roles in shaping public policy but also opens avenues for meaningful dialogue about future political cooperation and reform. It encourages a broader perspective on democratic governance and promotes the exchange of ideas that can strengthen political systems on both sides of the Atlantic. Ultimately, a deeper understanding of the strengths and weaknesses of different party systems is essential for building more effective and responsive democracies that can address the complex challenges of the 21st century.

THE OPEN SOCIETY DILEMMA
SOVEREIGNTY, INCLUSION AND GLOBAL GOVERNANCE

INTRODUCTION TO THE OPEN SOCIETY DILEMMA

Definition *of* Open Society

An open society is characterized by a commitment to democratic governance, individual freedoms, and the protection of human rights. At its core, the concept emphasizes transparency, accountability, and the rule of law, ensuring that citizens are actively engaged in the decision-making processes that affect their lives. This framework allows for the flourishing of diverse opinions, fostering a culture where dialogue and dissent are not only tolerated but encouraged. The open society model stands in contrast to more authoritarian or closed systems, which tend to suppress individual freedoms and limit participation in governance.

The philosophical roots of the open society can be traced to the works of thinkers like Karl Popper, who argued that societies should embrace critical discourse and adaptability to change. This adaptability is essential in a globalized world where rapid technological and social transformations challenge traditional governance structures. By promoting inclusivity and diversity, an open society aims to create environments where marginalized voices are heard, and policies reflect the varied experiences and needs of all citizens. This inclusiveness is vital to establishing social cohesion and mitigating the divisive effects of prejudice.

In the context of global governance, the open society paradigm intersects with the debates surrounding liberalism and federalism. While liberalism advocates for individual rights and freedoms on a global scale, federalism emphasizes the importance of local autonomy and the distribution of power among different governance levels. This intersection raises critical questions about how best to balance the need for global cooperation with the desire for local control. The challenge lies in creating systems that respect sovereignty while simultaneously promoting inclusive policies that acknowledge the rights and identities of diverse populations.

Sovereignty plays a dual role in this discussion, as it can both empower and hinder the promotion of inclusive policies. On one hand, the principle of sovereignty allows nations to uphold their cultural values and make decisions that reflect the will of their citizens. On the other hand, an overly rigid interpretation of sovereignty can lead to exclusionary practices that undermine human rights and global cooperation. As nations grapple with immigration and refugee challenges, the influence of liberal values becomes increasingly apparent. Policies that prioritize human dignity and acceptance often clash with national interests, revealing tensions that need careful navigation.

Ultimately, the quest for an open society is a balancing act that requires ongoing dialogue among stakeholders at all levels. Historical perspectives on federalism, sovereignty, and liberal thought provide valuable insights into how societies can cultivate environments that promote equality and acceptance while navigating the complexities of global governance. Case studies demonstrating the interplay between liberal and federalist approaches highlight the potential for collaboration in achieving shared goals, such as global peace and cooperation. By fostering an open society, nations can work towards solutions that not only respect individual rights but also enhance collective well-being in an interconnected world.

Overview *of* Sovereignty, Inclusion, *and* Global Governance

Sovereignty, inclusion, and global governance represent critical themes in contemporary discussions about the structure and function of societies worldwide. The principle of sovereignty traditionally emphasizes the authority of a state to govern itself without external interference. However, in an increasingly interconnected world, the dynamics of sovereignty are evolving, particularly as states grapple with the pressures of globalization. The tension between maintaining sovereign power and embracing a more inclusive approach that recognizes the rights and identities of diverse populations is at the heart of the discourse on global governance.

In the context of liberalism and federalism, the debate often centers on how to balance individual rights with collective governance. Liberalism advocates for the protection of individual freedoms and the promotion of equality, which can sometimes clash with the autonomous decision-making of sovereign states. Conversely, federalism offers a framework that encourages local governance while still adhering to broader national or international structures. This duality presents challenges and opportunities for crafting policies that are both inclusive and respectful of state sovereignty.

The impact of liberal values on immigration and refugee policies is a significant area of concern within this framework. Liberal principles often advocate for open borders and the humane treatment of migrants, emphasizing the importance of compassion and human rights. However, the sovereign rights of states to control their borders and determine who may enter can lead to conflicting policies that reflect varying degrees of inclusion. Analyzing these policies through the lens of both liberal and federalist perspectives reveals how states can navigate these complexities while striving for a more inclusive society.

Moreover, federalism can serve as a mechanism for promoting equality and acceptance by allowing for local governance that is more attuned to the needs and values of diverse communities. This localized approach can enhance social cohesion by empowering minority groups and fostering an environment where their voices can be heard. At the same time, it must be acknowledged that the principle of sovereignty can create barriers to effective cooperation and inclusion at the global level, particularly when states prioritize their own interests over collective well-being.

Historical perspectives on the interplay between federalism, sovereignty, and liberal thought reveal a complex range of ideas that inform current debates. The evolution of these concepts has been shaped by significant events and movements that have tested the limits of inclusion and the authority of states. Case studies illustrating the successes and failures of liberalism and federalism in promoting global peace and cooperation further underscore the importance of these themes. Understanding this complex landscape is essential for fostering an open society that champions both sovereignty and the principles of inclusion and acceptance.

LIBERALISM vs FEDERALISM

A COMPARATIVE FRAMEWORK

Key Principles *of* LIBERALISM

Liberalism, as a political philosophy, is founded on several key principles that emphasize individual freedom, equality, and the protection of human rights. At its core, liberalism advocates for a society where individuals can pursue their own interests while being protected from arbitrary authority. This principle of individual autonomy is essential in fostering an open society that values diversity and inclusion. By promoting personal freedoms, such as freedom of speech, religion, and association, liberalism seeks to create an environment where people can express themselves without fear of discrimination or persecution, thus laying the groundwork for policies that embrace multiculturalism and social cohesion. This commitment to individual liberty extends beyond mere tolerance; it actively encourages the flourishing of diverse perspectives, recognizing that a vibrant and dynamic society is one where individuals are empowered to contribute their unique talents and ideas. Furthermore, the emphasis on individual autonomy necessitates a limited government, one that respects the boundaries of personal freedom and avoids undue interference in private lives or economic activities. This is not to say that government has no role, but rather that its actions should be circumscribed by the need to protect individual rights and promote the common good in a way that minimizes intrusion on personal liberty.

Another fundamental principle of liberalism is the belief in equality before the law. This principle asserts that all individuals, regardless of their background, should have equal access to legal protections and opportunities. This includes the right to a fair trial, equal treatment under the justice system, and the absence of discrimination based on factors like race, gender, religion, or sexual orientation. In the context of global governance, this translates into policies that promote inclusivity and acceptance, particularly concerning immigration and refugee issues. By advocating for systems that recognize the rights of all individuals, liberalism facilitates the establishment of frameworks that prioritize human dignity and equality, challenging the barriers that often arise from nationalism and exclusivity. This commitment to equality extends beyond the legal realm, encompassing efforts to address social and economic disparities that may impede individual opportunity. Liberalism often advocates for policies such as progressive taxation, social safety nets, and investment in education and healthcare to create a more level playing field and ensure that all individuals have a fair chance to succeed.

The relationship between liberalism and sovereignty also plays a crucial role in shaping inclusive policies. While sovereignty traditionally emphasizes the autonomy of states, liberalism encourages a rethinking of this concept to advocate for global cooperation and shared responsibilities. This perspective allows for the promotion of inclusive governance structures that can address transnational challenges such as climate change, human rights violations, and economic inequality. By redefining sovereignty to include a commitment to global citizenship, liberalism fosters a collaborative approach where the rights of individuals are prioritized over the rigid boundaries of nation-states. This does not mean the abandonment of national sovereignty, but rather a recognition that certain global challenges require collective action and that states have a responsibility to cooperate in addressing them. This can manifest in international agreements, treaties, and organizations designed to promote human rights, environmental protection, and economic stability.

Liberal values significantly influence the development of immigration and refugee policies, advocating for humane treatment and the integration of migrants into society. These values are rooted in the recognition of shared humanity and the need for societies to benefit from the contributions of diverse populations. Liberal immigration policies tend to emphasize principles such as family reunification, skills-based immigration, and humanitarian protection for refugees and asylum seekers. In this sense, liberalism not only addresses the moral imperatives associated with refugee protection but also emphasizes the economic and cultural advantages of inclusive immigration policies. Immigrants often bring new skills, entrepreneurial spirit, and cultural perspectives that enrich society and contribute to economic growth. This principle aligns with the broader goals of fostering social cohesion and promoting equality within an increasingly interconnected world. However, liberalism also acknowledges the need for well-managed immigration systems that are fair, transparent, and responsive to the needs of both immigrants and host communities.

The intersection of economic policies and liberal ideals underscores the importance of creating open societies that promote equality and acceptance. Liberalism advocates for free markets and economic opportunities while also recognizing the need for regulations that protect vulnerable populations. This balance between economic freedom and social responsibility is essential for fostering environments where all individuals can thrive. While advocating for market-based solutions, liberalism also acknowledges the potential for market failures and the need for government intervention to address issues such as environmental protection, consumer safety, and income inequality. This includes policies such as antitrust regulations, environmental regulations, and social welfare programs. By examining historical perspectives on federalism and sovereignty through the lens of liberal thought, it becomes evident that the principles of liberalism can guide the development of effective governance structures that promote peace, cooperation, and inclusive policies on a global scale. The ongoing evolution of liberalism involves grappling with new challenges and adapting its core principles to address contemporary issues such as technological disruption, globalization, and rising inequality, ensuring its continued relevance in the 21st century. The core tenets of individual liberty, equality, and the rule of law remain foundational for building just and prosperous societies around the world.

Key Principles *of* FEDERALISM

Federalism stands as a time-tested governance model that accentuates the division of powers and responsibilities between national and regional authorities, striking a delicate balance between autonomy and inclusion. This intricate structure ensures that a diverse range of voices and interests are not only heard but actively represented, all while maintaining national coherence and unity. The principles of federalism hold particular significance in discussions of global governance, where the complex interplay between local autonomy and overarching national policies plays a pivotal role in achieving genuinely inclusive practices. By empowering local governments to tailor policies to the unique needs and characteristics of their populations, federalism fosters a strong sense of belonging and acceptance among diverse communities, promoting social harmony and cohesion.

At the heart of federalism lies the concept of shared sovereignty. In stark contrast to centralized systems where power is concentrated solely at the national level, a federal system meticulously distributes power among various tiers of government. This decentralization is not merely a structural arrangement; it is a deliberate strategy to enable more localized decision-making, ensuring that policies are crafted in direct response to the specific needs and values of individual communities. This localized approach enhances the relevance and effectiveness of governance, fostering a deeper connection between citizens and their government. By promoting shared sovereignty, federalism actively cultivates democratic engagement and encourages active participation from citizens at all levels, which is indispensable in an open society that cherishes inclusion and acceptance. Citizens are more likely to engage actively in governance when they feel their voices are heard and their concerns are addressed at a level that directly impacts their lives.

Another cornerstone of federalism is the protection of minority rights. Federal systems often incorporate mechanisms specifically designed to safeguard the interests of smaller or marginalized groups, ensuring that they have a meaningful voice in the political process. These mechanisms can include reserved seats in legislative bodies, constitutional protections for minority languages and cultures, and judicial review to ensure that laws do not disproportionately harm minority groups. This principle is particularly salient in the context of immigration and refugee policies, where federalism can provide a robust framework for addressing the inherent complexities of diversity. By recognizing the autonomy of local jurisdictions, federalism allows for the implementation of policies that are thoughtfully sensitive to the specific cultural and social dynamics of immigrant populations, thereby promoting social cohesion and harmony. Local governments can develop targeted programs and services that address the unique challenges faced by immigrant communities, such as language training, job placement assistance, and cultural integration initiatives.

Federalism proactively encourages economic collaboration among different regions, fostering a dynamic environment for tailored economic policies that address local needs while simultaneously contributing to national growth and prosperity. This principle is particularly pivotal in the context of liberal ideals, which ardently advocate for open markets and seamless economic integration. By facilitating economic cooperation, federalism plays a crucial role in bridging the gap between local and global economic interests, promoting equality and acceptance across various socioeconomic strata. This intricate interplay between economic policies and federal structures can lead to more equitable outcomes, particularly in societies striving for greater inclusion and opportunity for all. For example, federalism can enable states or provinces to experiment with different economic policies, such as different tax rates or regulatory frameworks, which can then be evaluated and potentially adopted at the national level if successful.

Finally, federalism serves as a vital framework for navigating the inherent tensions between human rights and sovereignty in the intricate landscape of global affairs. While sovereignty is often perceived as a shield against external interference, safeguarding a nation's autonomy, it can also pose formidable challenges to the promotion and protection of fundamental human rights. Federalism, with its unwavering emphasis on decentralization and local governance, provides a practical and effective pathway for addressing these challenges by allowing for the establishment of human rights protections at multiple levels of government. This layered approach can significantly enhance accountability and responsiveness to human rights concerns, ultimately fostering a more inclusive and just society. Local governments can enact their own human rights ordinances, establish human rights commissions, and provide legal aid to victims of human rights abuses. Through these key principles, federalism emerges as a compelling and adaptable model for advancing the ideals of an open society while effectively addressing the multifaceted complexities of sovereignty and inclusion in an increasingly interconnected world. Its ability to balance local autonomy with national unity, protect minority rights, foster economic collaboration, and navigate the tensions between human rights and sovereignty makes it a valuable framework for governance in diverse and dynamic societies. Moreover, the ongoing evolution and adaptation of federal systems around the world demonstrate their enduring relevance and potential for addressing contemporary challenges. As societies grapple with issues such as globalization, migration, and climate change, the principles of federalism offer a valuable roadmap for building more inclusive, just, and sustainable communities.

Tensions *and* Synergies Between Liberalism *and* Federalism

The relationship between liberalism and federalism is characterized by a complex interplay of tensions and synergies that shape the discourse on sovereignty and inclusion in global governance. Liberalism, with its emphasis on individual rights, personal freedoms, and the idea of an open society, often champions policies that promote inclusivity and multiculturalism. In contrast, federalism prioritizes the division of powers among various levels of government, fostering local autonomy and decision-making. This divergence can lead to friction, especially when local governments prioritize regional identities and interests that may conflict with national liberal ideals. However, this tension can also yield beneficial synergies, as federal structures can provide the flexibility needed to implement liberal policies that respect diversity while maintaining a commitment to human rights and equality.

Examining the role of sovereignty within this context reveals that it can be both a barrier and a facilitator of inclusive policies. Sovereignty is traditionally perceived as a state's authority over its territory and population, which can lead to exclusionary practices, particularly concerning immigration and refugee policies. Liberalism challenges this notion by advocating for the protection of individual rights regardless of national boundaries. The interaction between liberalism and federalism can be instrumental in redefining sovereignty to promote more inclusive policies. Federal systems can accommodate the need for local governance while enabling the implementation of broader liberal values, thus fostering an environment where diverse populations can coexist and thrive.

The impact of liberal values on immigration and refugee policies further illustrates the dynamic between these ideologies. Liberalism advocates for open borders and the protection of vulnerable populations, arguing that acceptance and inclusion are fundamental human rights. Federalism, on the other hand, may impose restrictions based on regional preferences or economic considerations. The challenge lies in balancing these competing interests to create immigration policies that uphold the principles of liberalism while respecting the autonomy of local governments. Case studies demonstrate that successful federal systems often adopt inclusive immigration practices that align with liberal values, thereby enhancing social cohesion and promoting a sense of belonging among diverse groups.

In exploring federalism's role in local governance, one can see how it serves as a framework for promoting equality and acceptance. Federal structures can empower local authorities to devise tailored solutions that reflect the unique needs of their communities, fostering a sense of ownership and participation among residents. This localized approach can enhance the effectiveness of policies aimed at promoting social inclusion and equality, as local governments are often more attuned to the specific challenges faced by marginalized groups. By integrating liberal ideals into federal governance, societies can work towards reducing disparities and creating environments where all individuals feel valued and included.

The intersection of economic policies and liberal ideals also highlights the tensions and synergies present in the relationship between liberalism and federalism. Liberalism often emphasizes free markets and individual entrepreneurship, which can sometimes conflict with the federalist approach of regulating economic activity at various levels. However, when federal systems prioritize inclusive economic policies that reflect liberal principles, they can stimulate growth while ensuring that the benefits are equitably distributed. Historical perspectives on this relationship underscore the importance of adapting governance structures to promote both economic efficiency and social justice, ultimately contributing to a more cohesive and harmonious society in an increasingly interconnected world.

THE ROLE OF SOVEREIGNTY IN PROMOTING INCLUSIVE POLICIES

The Concept of Sovereignty

The concept of sovereignty remains a critical pillar in the discourse surrounding global governance, particularly in the context of liberalism and federalism. Sovereignty refers to the authority of a state to govern itself and make decisions free from external interference. This principle has historically shaped political landscapes, influencing how nations interact, formulate policies, and assert their identities on the global stage. In a world increasingly characterized by interdependence and globalization, the traditional notion of sovereignty faces challenges, prompting a reevaluation of its implications for fostering inclusive societies.

Liberalism advocates for individual rights, freedoms, and equality, often promoting open societies that embrace diversity and multiculturalism. However, the commitment to sovereignty can complicate these ideals. States may prioritize their sovereignty to control immigration and refugee policies, often leading to exclusionary practices that conflict with the liberal values of acceptance and inclusiveness. The tension between safeguarding national interests and adhering to human rights norms becomes particularly pronounced in the context of migration, where the principles of liberalism and the realities of sovereignty must be balanced.

In contrast, federalism offers an alternative approach that can enhance inclusion and local governance. By distributing power among various levels of government, federal systems can provide a framework for addressing the unique needs of diverse populations while maintaining a degree of autonomy. This structure allows for the implementation of localized policies that reflect the values and aspirations of communities, promoting social cohesion and acceptance. Federalism, therefore, can act as a catalyst for equality by enabling marginalized groups to have a voice in governance processes, thus reinforcing the overarching goals of inclusivity.

The interplay between human rights and sovereignty introduces further complexity into global affairs. While sovereignty is often invoked to justify state actions, it can also serve as a barrier to the enforcement of international human rights standards. Navigating these tensions requires a nuanced understanding of how sovereignty can coexist with a commitment to human rights. For instance, states may assert their sovereignty in resisting external pressures to adopt inclusive policies, yet such resistance can lead to violations of fundamental rights. A careful examination of these dynamics is essential for fostering a global environment that respects both state sovereignty and individual dignity.

The historical perspectives on federalism, sovereignty, and liberal thought reveal an evolving narrative that underscores the importance of context in shaping governance frameworks. Case studies illustrate how different nations have navigated the challenges posed by sovereignty while striving for peace and cooperation on the global stage. By analyzing various approaches, it becomes evident that striking a balance between sovereignty and inclusivity is not only possible but necessary for advancing human rights and fostering open societies. This balance will ultimately determine the effectiveness of global governance in addressing contemporary challenges while promoting a world that values both autonomy and acceptance.

Sovereignty *and* National Identity

Sovereignty and national identity are critical concepts that interact in complex ways within the framework of global governance. In liberal democracies, sovereignty often emphasizes the autonomy of the state, allowing it to define its own national identity and pursue policies reflecting its cultural values and historical experiences. This sense of identity can foster a strong bond among citizens, promoting social cohesion and a shared vision for the nation's future. However, this strong emphasis on sovereignty may also lead to exclusionary practices that challenge the principles of inclusion and acceptance that many liberal thinkers advocate.

The interplay between liberalism and federalism offers a distinct perspective on how sovereignty can be utilized to promote inclusive policies. Federalism, with its decentralization of power, allows for a more nuanced approach to governance where local identities can flourish within a broader national framework. This structure can enhance the representation of diverse communities, enabling them to participate in decision-making processes that affect their lives directly. As a result, federal systems may better accommodate varying cultural identities while maintaining the integrity of national sovereignty.

The impact of liberal values on immigration and refugee policies further illustrates the tension between sovereignty and national identity. Liberal ideologies typically champion human rights and the protection of vulnerable populations, advocating for open borders and inclusive practices. Yet, the assertion of national sovereignty often leads to restrictive immigration policies aimed at preserving a particular national identity. This presents a dilemma where nations struggle to balance their commitment to liberal humanitarian principles with the desire to maintain control over their borders and uphold a cohesive national identity.

Federalism can also serve as a framework for promoting equality and acceptance in diverse societies. By allowing different regions or states to create tailored policies that reflect the unique needs and identities of their populations, federal systems can reduce tensions associated with cultural homogeneity. This local governance model enables communities to embrace their distinctiveness while contributing to the overarching goals of national unity and social harmony. The challenge lies in ensuring that these local policies do not reinforce divisions but rather foster a spirit of cooperation and mutual respect among various cultural groups.

Historical perspectives on federalism, sovereignty, and liberal thought reveal that these concepts have evolved over time, influenced by shifting political landscapes and social movements. Case studies of liberalism and federalism highlight their roles in promoting global peace and cooperation, illustrating how well-managed sovereignty can lead to successful collaborations among nations. As societies continue to grapple with issues of identity in an increasingly interconnected world, the dialogue surrounding sovereignty and national identity remains crucial in shaping inclusive and equitable governance frameworks that respect both individual rights and collective identities.

Challenges *to* Sovereignty *in an* Open Society

In an open society, the concept of sovereignty faces significant challenges, particularly in the context of globalization and the increasing interconnectedness of nations. The tension between liberalism and federalism emerges as a central theme in understanding these challenges. Liberalism, with its emphasis on individual rights and freedoms, advocates for an open world that embraces diversity and promotes inclusive policies. However, this ideal often conflicts with the notion of sovereignty, which prioritizes the authority and autonomy of states. As societies grapple with the implications of open governance, the need to balance these competing ideologies becomes paramount.

One of the primary challenges to sovereignty in an open society arises from the complexities of immigration and refugee policies. Liberal values promote the acceptance and inclusion of individuals regardless of their background, yet this can strain the existing frameworks of national sovereignty. States are tasked with maintaining their borders and ensuring the welfare of their citizens while also adhering to humanitarian principles. This dual obligation can lead to tensions, as nations must navigate the fine line between protecting their sovereignty and fulfilling their moral responsibilities to those in need. The result is often a contentious political landscape where policies are scrutinized for their effectiveness and fairness.

Federalism offers a potential solution to the challenges posed by an open society by providing a framework for balancing autonomy and inclusion. Through decentralized governance, federal systems can empower local authorities to address the unique needs of diverse populations while maintaining a cohesive national policy. This approach allows for greater adaptability in implementing inclusive policies that resonate with local communities, ultimately enhancing social cohesion. However, the effectiveness of federalism in promoting equality and acceptance depends on the willingness of various levels of government to collaborate and prioritize the common good over partisan interests.

The intersection of human rights and sovereignty further complicates the dialogue surrounding open societies. While liberalism champions the protection of human rights as a fundamental principle, the assertion of state sovereignty can lead to the infringement of these rights, particularly in instances where governments prioritize national interests over individual freedoms. Navigating these tensions requires a nuanced understanding of how global governance can uphold human rights without undermining the authority of states. In this context, the role of international organizations becomes critical, as they can advocate for the protection of human rights while respecting the sovereignty of nations.

Ultimately, the challenges to sovereignty in an open society reflect broader historical and ideological currents. The evolution of federalism and liberalism has shaped contemporary debates about global governance, multiculturalism, and social cohesion. Case studies reveal that while both ideologies present unique strengths and weaknesses, their interplay can foster environments conducive to peace and cooperation. As societies continue to confront the dilemmas of inclusion and acceptance, a comprehensive understanding of these dynamics will be essential for crafting policies that honor both sovereignty and the fundamental values of an open society.

THE IMPACT OF LIBERAL VALUES ON IMMIGRATION AND REFUGEE POLICIES

Liberal Ideals *and* Immigration

Liberal ideals, rooted in principles of individual freedom, equality, and justice, have profoundly influenced immigration policies across the globe. Advocates for liberal immigration policies often argue for an open society where individuals, regardless of their origin, possess the right to seek refuge and opportunity. These ideals emphasize the intrinsic value of diversity, positing that multicultural societies enrich the social fabric and contribute to economic vitality. By promoting inclusion and acceptance, liberalism seeks to dismantle prejudices that have historically marginalized certain groups, thus fostering an environment conducive to mutual respect and shared prosperity.

In contrast, the concept of sovereignty often presents challenges for liberal immigration policies. Sovereignty, which prioritizes the authority of nation-states to control borders and dictate citizenship, can clash with the liberal aspiration of an open world. This tension becomes evident in debates surrounding national security, economic stability, and cultural identity. While some argue that unrestricted immigration undermines national sovereignty, others contend that a commitment to human rights and the protection of vulnerable populations should guide immigration policies. This discourse highlights the complexities of balancing state autonomy with the moral imperative to offer sanctuary to those in need.

The role of federalism emerges as a critical factor in mediating the relationship between liberal ideals and immigration. Federal systems, which distribute power across multiple levels of government, can create avenues for local jurisdictions to adopt inclusive immigration policies that align with liberal values. In this framework, local governments have the autonomy to enact measures that foster acceptance and integration, often reflecting the unique cultural and demographic contexts of their communities. This decentralized approach allows for a more nuanced response to immigration, enabling localities to address the specific needs of immigrants while also engaging with broader national policies.

Liberal values significantly shape the discourse surrounding immigration and refugee policies, advocating for approaches that prioritize human rights and social justice. These values have led to the establishment of frameworks that seek to ensure equitable treatment for immigrants and refugees, emphasizing dignity and protection against discrimination. However, the effectiveness of these policies often hinges on the political will and commitment of federal and local authorities to uphold liberal principles, which can vary significantly across different regions. Therefore, the interplay between liberal values and the implementation of immigration policies remains a dynamic and evolving landscape.

The intersection of economic policies and liberal ideals further complicates the immigration debate. Economic arguments for immigration often highlight the contributions of immigrants to labor markets, innovation, and cultural dynamism. Yet, fears of economic displacement and competition can incite resistance against liberal immigration policies. Thus, it becomes essential to consider how federalism can serve as a framework for promoting equality and acceptance, allowing for policies that not only acknowledge the economic benefits of immigration but also address the concerns of local populations. By fostering a dialogue that integrates economic realities with liberal ideals, societies can work towards more inclusive and sustainable immigration practices.

Refugee Policies *across* Liberal Democracies

Refugee policies across liberal democracies present a complex interplay between the ideals of inclusivity and the realities of national sovereignty. Liberal democracies often espouse values such as human rights, equality, and multiculturalism, which theoretically support the acceptance and integration of refugees. However, the practical application of these values can vary significantly based on the political, economic, and social contexts within each nation. This subchapter will explore how different liberal democracies navigate the challenges of refugee policies while balancing their commitments to openness and the imperatives of sovereignty.

The impact of liberal values on immigration and refugee policies is profound, as these principles often advocate for humanitarian responses to crises. Countries like Canada and Sweden exemplify liberal democracies that have adopted relatively welcoming policies toward refugees, often citing moral obligations and historical legacies of immigration. These nations have implemented frameworks that facilitate refugee integration through access to education, healthcare, and employment. However, the increasing pressures of populism and nationalism within various liberal democracies have led to more restrictive policies, highlighting a growing tension between liberal ideals and practical governance.

Federalism plays a crucial role in shaping how refugee policies are enacted at the local level. In federal systems, states or provinces often have significant autonomy in determining their approach to refugee resettlement and integration. For instance, in Australia, states such as Victoria have pursued more inclusive measures, while others have adopted stricter protocols. This divergence illustrates the potential for federalism to simultaneously promote local autonomy and national coherence, creating a patchwork of policies that can either enhance or hinder the overall effectiveness of refugee integration efforts.

Navigating the tensions between human rights and sovereignty remains a critical challenge for liberal democracies. While international human rights frameworks advocate for the protection of refugees, states often prioritize their sovereignty in decision-making processes. This can lead to scenarios where countries impose stringent border controls and asylum processes, undermining their commitments to human rights. The interplay between these two spheres raises important questions about the moral responsibilities of liberal democracies in the global context and the implications of their choices on international norms and cooperation.

Ultimately, the intersection of economic policies and liberal ideals significantly influences refugee integration in open societies. Economic arguments for accepting refugees often emphasize the potential contributions of migrants to labor markets and demographic rejuvenation. However, the integration process can be complex and fraught with challenges, such as public resistance and resource allocation concerns. Understanding the historical perspectives on federalism, sovereignty, and liberal thought provides valuable insights into the contemporary debates surrounding refugee policies, illustrating the need for a balanced approach that promotes both inclusion and the legitimate interests of sovereign states.

CASE STUDIES OF SUCCESSFUL INCLUSION STRATEGIES

In examining successful inclusion strategies, it is crucial to highlight case studies that embody the principles of both liberalism and federalism. One notable example is Canada's multicultural policy, which promotes the coexistence of diverse cultural identities within a federal framework. This policy not only recognizes the rights of various ethnic groups but also actively encourages their participation in the political and social spheres. By fostering an environment where cultural pluralism is celebrated, Canada demonstrates how a federal system can effectively support inclusion while maintaining national cohesion. The Canadian experience underscores the importance of government structures that allow for localized decision-making, enabling communities to address their unique needs while contributing to a broader national identity.

Another significant case study is the European Union's approach to immigration and refugee policies. The EU employs a combination of supranational governance and member-state autonomy, aiming to create a unified response to migration challenges while respecting individual state sovereignty. The implementation of the Common European Asylum System reflects an effort to harmonize standards for refugee protection, ensuring that those in need find safety across member states. This model illustrates how federalism can facilitate both the protection of human rights and the management of immigration, presenting a balanced approach to inclusion that respects the diverse political landscapes of its member nations.

The experience of South Africa in the post-apartheid era further exemplifies effective inclusion strategies. The country's transition to a democratic federal system allowed for the establishment of a constitution that enshrines human rights and promotes social equity. South Africa's commitment to affirmative action policies aims to rectify historical injustices and foster greater inclusion of marginalized communities. This case study highlights the potential of federalism to address social disparities while empowering local governments to tailor policies that reflect the needs of their constituents. The South African model serves as a reminder that inclusive policies must be adaptive and responsive to the dynamic nature of societal needs.

In the realm of economic inclusion, the Nordic countries provide a compelling case study. These nations have successfully integrated liberal economic policies with robust social welfare systems, ensuring that economic growth translates into broad-based prosperity. By prioritizing social equity and promoting equal opportunities through education and labor market policies, the Nordic model exemplifies how economic frameworks can align with liberal values to create inclusive societies. This approach not only enhances social cohesion but also fosters a sense of belonging among diverse populations, demonstrating that economic policies can be leveraged to support inclusion and acceptance.

Lastly, the case of New Zealand illustrates the integration of indigenous rights within a framework of federalism and liberal governance. The Treaty of Waitangi established a legal basis for recognizing the rights of the Māori people, promoting their active participation in governance and decision-making processes. This case study showcases how federalism can serve as a platform for empowering marginalized communities while balancing national interests. New Zealand's commitment to inclusivity highlights the necessity of incorporating diverse voices in the governance process, ultimately contributing to a more cohesive and harmonious society. Through these case studies, it becomes evident that successful inclusion strategies often require a delicate balance between liberal ideals and federal governance, paving the way for a more open and accepting world.

FEDERALISM AND LOCAL GOVERNANCE

BALANCING AUTONOMY AND INCLUSION

The Structure *of* Federal Governance

The structure of federal governance serves as a vital framework for understanding the relationship between sovereignty and inclusion in contemporary society. Federalism, characterized by the division of powers between central and regional governments, provides a unique approach to governance that can accommodate diverse populations while promoting democratic values. This dual structure allows for localized decision-making, which can enhance the responsiveness of governmental policies to the specific needs of various communities. In contrast, the liberal perspective emphasizes individual rights and freedoms, often advocating for a more centralized approach to governance that prioritizes universal human rights over regional autonomy.

In assessing the role of sovereignty within federal governance, it becomes clear that sovereignty can be both a facilitator and a barrier to inclusive policies. On one hand, the sovereignty of individual states allows them to tailor their policies to better serve their populations, fostering a sense of belonging and acceptance among diverse groups. On the other hand, an overemphasis on state sovereignty can lead to isolationist tendencies, where nations prioritize their interests at the expense of global cooperation. This tension highlights the necessity for a balanced approach that respects the autonomy of states while simultaneously acknowledging the interconnectedness of global challenges.

Liberal values significantly influence immigration and refugee policies, shaping how nations respond to the needs of displaced populations. In liberal democracies, the emphasis on human rights often translates into policies that prioritize the protection of refugees and the promotion of multiculturalism. However, the application of these values can vary significantly between federal systems, where local governments may adopt more restrictive or welcoming stances based on regional attitudes toward immigration. This interplay between liberal ideals and federalism illustrates the complexity of creating cohesive policies that align with both national interests and humanitarian obligations.

Federalism also plays a crucial role in balancing autonomy and inclusion within local governance. By allowing regions to exercise a degree of self-governance, federal systems can empower marginalized communities and promote social cohesion. Local governments can implement policies that reflect the unique cultural and social dynamics of their populations, thereby fostering an environment of acceptance and equality. However, this localized autonomy must be carefully managed to ensure that it does not lead to fragmentation or the exclusion of minority groups, highlighting the need for oversight and collaboration between different levels of government.

In examining the intersection of economic policies with liberal ideals in open societies, federal governance emerges as a vital mechanism for promoting equality and acceptance. Economic disparities often exacerbate social tensions, and federal systems can implement targeted economic policies that address these inequalities while promoting inclusivity. This approach requires a commitment to human rights and social justice, ensuring that economic growth benefits all segments of society. Historical perspectives on federalism reveal that successful models often incorporate lessons from previous governance structures, adapting them to meet the evolving needs of diverse populations in an increasingly interconnected world. Through case studies of liberalism and federalism, it becomes evident that both frameworks can contribute to global peace and cooperation, provided they are applied with a focus on inclusion and respect for human dignity.

Local Autonomy *and* Community Engagement

Local autonomy and community engagement play a critical role in the interplay between liberalism and federalism, particularly in the context of global governance. The concept of local autonomy refers to the power and capacity of local governments and communities to self-govern and make decisions that reflect their unique needs and values. In a federal system, this autonomy is essential for balancing the interests of diverse populations while ensuring that local voices are heard within the broader framework of national and international policies. This dynamic becomes increasingly relevant as societies seek to promote inclusion and acceptance in an open world, where the challenges of globalization often lead to tensions between local identities and overarching national or global imperatives.

Engagement at the community level fosters a sense of belonging and participation that is vital for the health of democratic societies. Through local governance structures, citizens can actively participate in decision-making processes that affect their lives, thus strengthening social cohesion. Federalism, by design, allows for such participation at multiple levels of government, enabling local communities to address their specific concerns while cooperating with national authorities to achieve broader objectives. The challenge lies in ensuring that this engagement does not lead to exclusionary practices but rather promotes a culture of inclusivity that embraces diversity and mitigates prejudices.

The relationship between local autonomy and sovereignty is particularly significant when considering policies on immigration and refugee resettlement. Liberal values often advocate for open borders and humanitarian assistance, while sovereignty emphasizes the rights of states to control their territories and populations. Local governments, empowered by autonomy, can play a pivotal role in shaping inclusive immigration policies that reflect the values of their communities. By engaging residents in dialogue about the benefits and challenges of immigration, local leaders can promote understanding and acceptance, fostering a climate where newcomers are welcomed and integrated rather than marginalized.

Furthermore, the impact of federalism on local governance is evident in its ability to balance the need for local autonomy with the imperatives of national unity. Federal systems can provide the framework necessary for promoting equality and acceptance by allowing diverse communities to maintain their cultural identities while contributing to the common good. This balance is crucial in addressing the concerns of minority groups who may feel threatened by dominant narratives. In this regard, the role of local engagement becomes even more pronounced as communities work collaboratively to create policies that reflect shared values while respecting individual differences.

Ultimately, the intersection of local autonomy and community engagement within the context of sovereignty and global governance highlights the complexities of fostering an open society. Striking a balance between the principles of liberalism and federalism requires an ongoing commitment to dialogue, understanding, and cooperation. By prioritizing local voices in governance processes, societies can navigate the tensions inherent in global affairs, promoting human rights and social cohesion while embracing the diversity that enriches the human experience. In doing so, they can pave the way for a more inclusive and equitable future, where both local and global aspirations can coexist harmoniously.

Inclusion Strategies *at* Local Levels

Inclusion strategies at local levels are essential for fostering an open society that embraces diversity and promotes equality. Local governance plays a crucial role in implementing inclusive policies that reflect the values of liberalism while respecting the principles of federalism and sovereignty. By prioritizing community engagement and participatory governance, local authorities can create environments where all citizens, regardless of their background, feel valued and included. This approach not only enhances social cohesion but also strengthens the democratic fabric of society, making it imperative for policymakers to consider the nuances of local contexts when designing inclusion strategies. Moreover, the success of these strategies hinges on a multi-faceted approach that addresses social, economic, and political dimensions, ensuring that inclusion is more than just a concept but a lived reality for all residents.

One effective strategy for promoting inclusion at the local level is the establishment of community advisory boards that represent diverse populations. These boards can provide insights into the unique needs and challenges faced by various groups, ensuring that local policies are not only equitable but also responsive to the realities of marginalized communities. By incorporating the perspectives of minority groups, local governments can address issues such as access to services, housing, and employment, which are critical for fostering an inclusive environment. This model aligns with liberal ideals that emphasize the importance of representation and participation in the decision-making process, ultimately leading to more effective governance. The composition of such boards should reflect the demographic makeup of the community, including representation from racial and ethnic minorities, religious groups, LGBTQ+ individuals, people with disabilities, and other underrepresented populations. Furthermore, these boards should be given meaningful authority and resources to influence policy decisions and hold local governments accountable for their commitments to inclusion. Regular public forums and town hall meetings can also provide additional avenues for community input and feedback.

Another key aspect of inclusion strategies is the development of tailored educational programs that promote multicultural understanding and acceptance. Local governments can partner with schools, community organizations, and cultural institutions to offer workshops and events that celebrate diversity and encourage dialogue among different cultural groups. Such initiatives not only enhance social cohesion but also combat prejudice and discrimination, aligning with the broader liberal commitment to human rights. By investing in education and community building, local authorities can cultivate a culture of acceptance that resonates beyond their immediate jurisdictions. These educational programs should not be limited to schools but should also be offered to local businesses, government employees, and the broader community. Topics covered might include cultural sensitivity training, implicit bias awareness, conflict resolution, and the history and contributions of different cultural groups. Moreover, local libraries can serve as valuable resources for promoting multiculturalism by offering diverse collections, hosting author talks and cultural events, and providing access to technology and information for all residents.

Moreover, the intersection of economic policies and inclusion cannot be overstated. Local governments can leverage economic development initiatives to create job opportunities for underrepresented populations, thereby promoting economic inclusion. Policies that support small businesses owned by minorities or immigrants, for example, can be instrumental in reducing economic disparities and fostering a sense of belonging within the community. By integrating economic empowerment with inclusion strategies, local governance can address the root causes of inequality and contribute to a more equitable society. This can involve targeted job training programs, mentorship opportunities, access to capital for minority-owned businesses, and incentives for companies to hire individuals from underrepresented groups. Local governments can also use their purchasing power to support businesses that prioritize diversity and inclusion in their hiring practices and supply chains. Furthermore, affordable housing initiatives and anti-poverty programs can help to ensure that all residents have access to basic necessities and opportunities for economic advancement.

Addressing systemic biases within local institutions is paramount. This requires a critical examination of policies and practices across various sectors, including law enforcement, education, and healthcare. Local governments must actively work to eliminate discriminatory practices and promote equitable outcomes for all residents. For example, police departments can implement community policing strategies, provide implicit bias training for officers, and establish civilian oversight boards to enhance accountability. Schools can adopt culturally responsive curricula, address achievement gaps, and create welcoming environments for students from diverse backgrounds. Healthcare providers can improve access to services for marginalized communities, address health disparities, and provide culturally competent care. Regular audits and evaluations can help to identify areas where systemic biases persist and inform the development of targeted interventions.

It is essential to recognize the role of federalism in shaping local inclusion strategies. While local governments have the autonomy to implement inclusive policies, they must also navigate the complexities of federal mandates and regulations. This delicate balance requires collaboration between different levels of government to ensure that inclusion efforts are not undermined by overarching policies that may prioritize sovereignty over social equity. By fostering a cooperative relationship between federal and local authorities, the principles of both liberalism and federalism can be harmonized to create a more inclusive framework for governance that truly reflects the values of an open society. This collaboration can take various forms, such as joint funding for inclusion initiatives, technical assistance from federal agencies, and regular consultations between federal and local officials. It is also important to recognize that federal laws and policies can sometimes create barriers to inclusion at the local level, and local governments should advocate for changes to these laws and policies to better align with their own inclusion goals.

Fostering inclusion at the local level requires a comprehensive and multi-faceted approach that addresses social, economic, and political dimensions. By establishing community advisory boards, developing tailored educational programs, promoting economic empowerment, addressing systemic biases, and fostering collaboration between federal and local authorities, local governments can create environments where all citizens feel valued, respected, and included. These efforts not only enhance social cohesion but also strengthen the democratic fabric of society, making it imperative for policymakers to prioritize inclusion strategies in their decision-making processes. Ultimately, the success of these strategies depends on a sustained commitment to creating a more equitable and just society for all.

HUMAN RIGHTS AND SOVEREIGNTY

NAVIGATING TENSIONS IN GLOBAL AFFAIRS

The Interplay of Human Rights and Sovereignty

The relationship between human rights and sovereignty is a complex and multifaceted issue that has garnered significant attention in contemporary global discourse. Sovereignty, defined as the authority of a state to govern itself and make its own laws, often comes into conflict with the universal principles of human rights that advocate for the protection and dignity of individuals regardless of national boundaries. This tension is particularly pronounced when states prioritize their sovereignty while undermining fundamental human rights, raising critical questions about the efficacy of global governance structures designed to promote both. The interplay of these two concepts necessitates a careful examination of how they can coexist harmoniously in an increasingly interconnected world.

The foundations of this intricate relationship can be traced back to the emergence of the modern nation-state system, enshrined in the Treaty of Westphalia in 1648. This treaty established the principle of state sovereignty, granting each state the right to non-interference in its internal affairs. However, the atrocities of the 20th century, particularly the Holocaust, prompted a re-evaluation of the absolute nature of sovereignty. The Universal Declaration of Human Rights in 1948 marked a turning point, signaling a global commitment to upholding fundamental rights, even within the confines of national borders. This declaration initiated a gradual but persistent shift towards a more conditional understanding of sovereignty, one that recognized the international community's responsibility to intervene in cases of gross human rights violations.

Liberalism, with its emphasis on individual freedoms and equality, promotes the idea that human rights are inherent to all people and should transcend national borders. This worldview challenges traditional notions of sovereignty by arguing that states cannot claim absolute authority over their citizens if they violate their rights. Liberal thinkers such as John Locke and Immanuel Kant have long championed the idea that governments derive their legitimacy from the consent of the governed and that the protection of individual rights is paramount. This perspective has fueled the development of international human rights law and institutions, which aim to hold states accountable for their treatment of their citizens.

In contrast, federalism, which advocates for a division of powers between central and regional governments, offers a different perspective. It allows for the accommodation of diverse groups within a state while maintaining a degree of sovereignty. This framework can facilitate inclusive policies that respect human rights, as it encourages local governance to address the unique needs of various communities while still adhering to overarching human rights standards. By decentralizing power, federal systems can empower regions to implement human rights protections that are tailored to their specific contexts, fostering a greater sense of ownership and legitimacy.

The impact of liberal values on immigration and refugee policies further illustrates the tension between human rights and sovereignty. In liberal democracies, the commitment to human rights often leads to more open immigration policies that prioritize the protection of vulnerable populations, such as refugees fleeing persecution and asylum seekers. The principle of non-refoulement, which prohibits states from returning refugees to countries where they face the risk of torture or persecution, is a cornerstone of international refugee law and reflects the influence of liberal values. However, these policies can sometimes clash with the notion of sovereignty when governments face pressures to regulate borders, manage national security, and address concerns about economic strain or social integration. The rise of nationalist and populist movements in recent years has intensified these tensions, leading to calls for stricter immigration controls and a more restrictive interpretation of refugee law. As states navigate these competing demands, the challenge lies in crafting policies that uphold human rights while respecting the authority of sovereign states. This balancing act is crucial for fostering an open society that values inclusion and acceptance.

Federalism can play a significant role in promoting inclusive policies that respect both human rights and sovereignty. By decentralizing power, federal systems can empower local governments to tailor their policies to better align with the needs and values of their communities. This approach not only enhances the autonomy of diverse groups but also encourages participation in governance, fostering a sense of belonging and social cohesion. For example, in a country with a diverse ethnic or religious makeup, a federal system might allow different regions to adopt laws that protect the rights of minority groups or promote cultural preservation. When local authorities are given the tools to address human rights issues pertinent to their constituents, they can create environments that support equality and acceptance, bridging the gap between individual rights and national sovereignty. However, it is crucial to ensure that decentralization does not lead to a race to the bottom, where regions compete to offer the lowest level of human rights protection in order to attract investment or appease certain constituencies.

The European Union provides a compelling example of the ongoing negotiation between human rights and sovereignty. Member states have voluntarily ceded some of their sovereignty to the EU in exchange for the benefits of economic integration and political cooperation. The EU has a strong commitment to human rights, enshrined in the Charter of Fundamental Rights, which applies to all EU institutions and member states when they are implementing EU law. The European Court of Human Rights, although not formally part of the EU, plays a vital role in upholding human rights across Europe, including in EU member states. However, the EU's human rights policies have faced challenges in recent years, particularly in the context of the refugee crisis and the rise of populism. The debate over border controls, asylum policies, and the treatment of migrants has exposed deep divisions within the EU and raised questions about the balance between national sovereignty and European-level human rights obligations.

Navigating the interplay of human rights and sovereignty requires an ongoing dialogue between different governance models. The historical perspectives on federalism, sovereignty, and liberal thought reveal that these concepts are not mutually exclusive but can be integrated to promote global peace and cooperation. Case studies demonstrate that successful governance often hinges on the ability to harmonize local autonomy with global human rights commitments. International organizations, such as the United Nations, play a crucial role in facilitating this dialogue, setting standards, and providing a forum for states to address human rights challenges collectively. However, the effectiveness of these organizations is often limited by the principle of state sovereignty, which gives states the right to refuse to comply with international norms and decisions.

In this context, a reimagined understanding of sovereignty that embraces the protection of human rights can lead to a more inclusive and equitable world, where the complexities of global governance are met with innovative solutions that honor both individual dignity and the authority of states. This requires a shift from a purely state-centric view of sovereignty to a more people-centered approach, one that recognizes that the legitimacy of a state ultimately depends on its ability to protect and promote the human rights of its citizens. This also necessitates strengthening international mechanisms for accountability and enforcement, while respecting the principle of subsidiarity, which holds that decisions should be taken at the lowest possible level of government. By fostering a global culture of human rights and promoting a more cooperative approach to sovereignty, we can move towards a world where the protection of human dignity is not seen as a threat to state authority, but rather as its very foundation. The challenge lies in finding creative ways to bridge the gap between the ideals of human rights and the realities of state power, ensuring that the pursuit of sovereignty does not come at the expense of human dignity.

Case Studies *of* Human Rights Violations *and* Sovereign Claims

Human rights violations within the context of sovereign claims illustrate the complex interplay between governance structures and the protection of individual liberties. This subchapter examines specific case studies that highlight how differing approaches to sovereignty, liberalism, and federalism have influenced human rights outcomes. By analyzing instances such as the Rohingya crisis in Myanmar and the treatment of Uighurs in China, we can discern how national sovereignty can both protect and undermine human rights. These cases provide critical insights into the challenges and responsibilities states face in adhering to international human rights standards while asserting their sovereign rights.

The Rohingya crisis presents a stark example of how a nation's claim to sovereignty can lead to widespread human rights abuses. In Myanmar, the government's refusal to recognize the Rohingya as citizens has resulted in systemic discrimination, violence, and forced displacement. This situation raises questions about the limits of sovereignty when it comes to protecting vulnerable populations. The international community's response, which has included both condemnation and humanitarian aid, underscores the tension between respecting state sovereignty and the obligation to intervene in cases of egregious human rights violations. This case serves as a reminder that while sovereignty is a fundamental principle of international law, it should not be a shield for states to commit abuses.

In contrast, the situation of the Uighurs in China further complicates the discourse on human rights and sovereignty. The Chinese government has justified its actions in Xinjiang, including mass detentions and cultural assimilation campaigns, as necessary measures for national security and social stability. This justification raises critical questions about the role of federalism and local governance in promoting human rights. In a federal system, local governments can potentially advocate for the rights of marginalized communities, yet in China's unitary state structure, local autonomy is severely limited. This case illustrates how the centralization of power can lead to the erosion of individual rights, emphasizing the need for governance frameworks that promote inclusivity and protect human rights.

The comparative analysis of these case studies reveals that liberal values often clash with sovereign claims, especially when the latter is wielded to justify human rights violations. While liberalism advocates for the protection of individual rights and freedoms, it faces significant challenges in states that prioritize sovereignty over international norms. The international community must navigate these tensions carefully, balancing respect for sovereignty with the necessity of holding states accountable for their human rights obligations. This dynamic is critical in understanding how global governance can evolve to better address human rights issues while recognizing the principles of state sovereignty.

Ultimately, these case studies highlight the urgent need for a re-evaluation of how sovereignty is conceptualized in relation to human rights. A framework that integrates liberal ideals of inclusion and acceptance with a recognition of the importance of sovereignty could lead to more effective governance models. By fostering dialogue between liberal and federalist perspectives, states can work towards promoting equality, social cohesion, and the protection of human rights. This balanced approach is essential for creating an open society that respects both the autonomy of states and the rights of individuals, ensuring that the pursuit of sovereignty does not come at the expense of fundamental human dignity.

The Role *of* International Law *in* Addressing Tensions

International law plays a critical role in addressing tensions arising from the complex interplay of sovereignty, inclusion, and global governance. As the international community grapples with issues such as migration, human rights, and economic disparities, legal frameworks established by treaties, conventions, and customary law serve as essential instruments for mitigating conflicts. These laws create a baseline for acceptable behavior among nations, promoting accountability and fostering dialogue. By providing a structured approach to dispute resolution, international law helps to manage the conflicting interests of states while simultaneously advocating for human rights and inclusivity.

The tension between liberalism and federalism is particularly pronounced in the realm of international law. Liberalism emphasizes individual rights and freedoms, advocating for an open world where diversity is embraced, and every individual has a voice. In contrast, federalism focuses on the distribution of power between central and local authorities, often prioritizing state sovereignty and regional autonomy. International law, in its essence, seeks to bridge these paradigms by establishing norms that recognize both the need for strong sovereign states and the importance of upholding universal human rights. This duality allows for a framework wherein states can exercise their sovereignty while also committing to international obligations that promote inclusiveness and cooperation.

Addressing issues such as immigration and refugee policies through the lens of international law underscores its vital role in fostering a more inclusive global society. Legal instruments, such as the 1951 Refugee Convention, delineate the responsibilities of states to protect individuals fleeing persecution. By adhering to these international commitments, countries can balance national interests with humanitarian obligations, thereby promoting social cohesion and acceptance. This legal framework not only safeguards the rights of displaced persons but also encourages host nations to adopt policies that facilitate integration and mutual respect among diverse populations.

The role of international law extends into the realm of federalism, where local governance must align with broader legal standards. Federalism often allows regions to enact policies that reflect their unique cultures and values, yet these policies must coexist with international norms that promote equality and human rights. The challenge lies in ensuring that local autonomy does not undermine the inclusivity mandated by international law. Through mechanisms such as the principle of subsidiarity, international law can guide federal systems in crafting policies that respect local governance while still adhering to global standards of equality and acceptance.

In conclusion, the interplay between international law and the tensions surrounding sovereignty and inclusion is pivotal for achieving global cooperation and peace. As nations navigate the complexities of liberal ideals and federal structures, international law provides a foundational framework that encourages dialogue and compromise. By promoting adherence to shared legal principles, the global community can work towards a more inclusive society that not only respects the sovereignty of states but also champions the rights and dignity of all individuals. The ongoing challenge will be to ensure that these legal frameworks evolve in response to emerging global dynamics, fostering an open world that embraces diversity while upholding the values of justice and equality.

THE INFLUENCE OF LIBERALISM ON MULTICULTURALISM AND SOCIAL COHESION

Liberalism *and* Cultural Diversity

Liberalism fundamentally champions individual freedoms and human rights, advocating for a society where diversity is not only accepted but celebrated. This ideology posits that cultural diversity enriches societies by fostering innovation, creativity, and resilience. In the context of global governance, liberalism seeks to create frameworks that not only acknowledge but actively promote inclusion. The recognition of diverse identities is essential to the liberal agenda, as it aligns with the overarching value of ensuring that every individual has the opportunity to express their cultural identity without fear of repression or discrimination. However, this commitment to diversity often raises complex questions about the balance between national sovereignty and the global imperative for inclusive policies.

The relationship between liberalism and federalism presents a unique dynamic in addressing cultural diversity. Federalism, characterized by the distribution of power between central and regional authorities, offers a structure that can enhance local governance while respecting cultural autonomy. In a federal system, local governments can tailor policies that reflect the unique cultural and social needs of their communities, promoting an inclusive environment. Liberalism, on the other hand, advocates for universal principles of rights and freedoms that can sometimes clash with regional autonomy. This tension necessitates a careful analysis of how these two frameworks can coexist, ensuring that cultural diversity is preserved while also upholding the liberal commitment to individual rights.

Human rights serve as a pivotal intersection between liberalism and sovereignty, particularly in the realm of immigration and refugee policies. Liberal values emphasize the protection of individuals regardless of their national origin, advocating for humane treatment and inclusion of migrants and refugees. This approach often challenges traditional notions of sovereignty, as it calls for states to recognize their responsibilities to uphold human rights beyond their borders. Consequently, the impact of liberal ideals can be seen in the growing movements for more inclusive immigration policies that prioritize humanitarian considerations over rigid national interests. However, this liberal stance is met with resistance in certain sovereign contexts where national identity and security concerns take precedence over global humanitarian obligations.

Federalism offers a potential framework for addressing the challenges posed by cultural diversity in an increasingly interconnected world. By allowing for decentralized governance, federal systems can accommodate diverse cultural practices and beliefs while fostering social cohesion at the national level. This balance is crucial in preventing the marginalization of minority groups and promoting equality. The ability of local governments to enact policies that reflect the needs and values of their constituents can lead to a more harmonious coexistence of various cultural identities, promoting a sense of belonging among all citizens. However, this requires a commitment from federal structures to ensure that local autonomy does not devolve into exclusionary practices that undermine the principles of equality and acceptance.

In examining the influence of liberalism on multiculturalism, it becomes evident that the ideals of freedom and equality are crucial for fostering social cohesion in diverse societies. Liberalism encourages the recognition and celebration of different cultures, which can lead to more vibrant and inclusive communities. Yet, the challenge remains in navigating the tensions between maintaining a cohesive national identity and allowing for the flourishing of diverse cultural expressions. As global governance evolves, the interplay between liberal values and federal structures will continue to shape the discourse on cultural diversity, highlighting the necessity for policies that embrace inclusivity while respecting the principles of sovereignty. This ongoing dialogue will be essential in addressing the complexities of promoting global peace and cooperation in an era marked by both interdependence and cultural plurality.

Policies Promoting Multiculturalism

Policies promoting multiculturalism play a crucial role in shaping open societies that seek to balance inclusion and acceptance with the principles of sovereignty and governance. Within the context of liberalism and federalism, multicultural policies serve as instruments to foster social cohesion and respect for diversity. These policies are designed to recognize and celebrate cultural differences while simultaneously promoting the idea of a shared national identity. By doing so, they encourage coexistence among diverse groups, thus reinforcing the notion that an inclusive society can thrive on the foundations of mutual respect and understanding.

Liberal values have significantly influenced immigration and refugee policies, propelling nations towards embracing multiculturalism. Programs aimed at integrating immigrants into the social fabric of a host country often draw upon liberal ideals of equality and human rights. These policies typically emphasize the importance of providing equal opportunities for all individuals, regardless of their background. By facilitating access to education, healthcare, and employment for immigrants, liberal policies not only enhance social mobility but also contribute to the overall economic and cultural vitality of the society, demonstrating how multiculturalism can be an asset rather than a liability.

Federalism, on the other hand, offers a unique framework for promoting equality and inclusion at various levels of governance. By allowing local governments to tailor policies to the specific needs of their communities, federalism can enhance the effectiveness of multicultural initiatives. Local authorities often possess a better understanding of the demographic composition and cultural needs of their populations, enabling them to implement targeted programs that reflect the values and identities of diverse groups. This decentralized approach can lead to the successful integration of multicultural policies, fostering a sense of belonging among all citizens while respecting the autonomy of local governance.

The intersection of economic policies and liberal ideals is also essential in advancing multiculturalism. Economic opportunities that are accessible to all members of society can significantly reduce disparities and promote social cohesion. Policies that encourage entrepreneurship and support minority-owned businesses contribute to a more vibrant and diverse economy. Furthermore, when economic growth is inclusive, it helps to mitigate tensions that may arise from cultural differences, thus reinforcing the idea that an open society can benefit from the contributions of all its members, regardless of their cultural background.

In conclusion, the promotion of multiculturalism through thoughtful policies is vital for the development of open societies that prioritize inclusion while respecting sovereignty. By analyzing the interplay between liberalism and federalism, we can better understand how these frameworks influence global governance and the pursuit of social cohesion. Ultimately, the commitment to multicultural policies not only enriches the social fabric but also enhances the resilience of societies in facing the challenges of globalization, ensuring that diversity is celebrated as a cornerstone of democratic life.

Challenges *to* Social Cohesion *in* Diverse Societies

The challenges to social cohesion in diverse societies often stem from the inherent tensions between liberal ideals and the principles of federalism. In liberal democracies, the emphasis on individual rights and freedoms can sometimes clash with the need for collective identity and social cohesion. This dynamic is particularly evident in multicultural societies where the influx of various cultural, ethnic, and religious groups can lead to friction. The liberal focus on inclusivity may inadvertently overlook the importance of fostering a shared sense of belonging among diverse populations, thereby risking social fragmentation.

Federalism, on the other hand, offers a framework that can potentially bridge these divides by allowing for localized governance that respects the unique identities of different communities. However, this approach also faces challenges, as it can lead to uneven distribution of resources and attention, potentially fostering resentment among groups that feel marginalized. In practice, federal systems may struggle to balance the autonomy of local governments with the need for overarching policies that promote unity and social cohesion, complicating efforts to create inclusive societies.

The impact of liberal values on immigration and refugee policies further complicates this landscape. While liberalism advocates for the acceptance and integration of newcomers, it can also provoke resistance from segments of the population that fear cultural dilution or economic competition. This resistance can manifest in xenophobia and social discord, undermining the very principles of inclusivity that liberalism seeks to promote. The challenge lies in crafting policies that not only welcome diversity but also actively engage existing communities in the process of integration, ensuring that all voices are heard and valued.

Human rights considerations add another layer to the discussion of sovereignty and social cohesion. Nations often grapple with the tension between upholding their sovereignty and adhering to international human rights standards. This conflict can lead to policies that prioritize national interests over the rights of individuals from diverse backgrounds, resulting in social unrest and division. It is essential for states to navigate these tensions delicately, fostering an environment where human rights are respected while also maintaining the social fabric of the nation.

In conclusion, the intersection of liberalism, federalism, and social cohesion in diverse societies presents a complex array of challenges. Achieving a balance between respecting individual freedoms and fostering a unified community requires thoughtful governance that prioritizes inclusion and acceptance. Policymakers must be vigilant in addressing the fears and concerns of all constituents, ensuring that social cohesion is not sacrificed in the pursuit of liberal ideals. Through comparative analysis and case studies, it becomes evident that both liberalism and federalism must evolve to meet the needs of diverse societies, promoting harmony and cooperation in an increasingly interconnected world.

FEDERALISM AS A FRAMEWORK FOR PROMOTING EQUALITY AND ACCEPTANCE

The Federal Model *and* Equality

The federal model provides a unique framework for addressing the complexities of equality within the context of global governance. By distributing power across various levels of government, federalism allows for the tailoring of policies that reflect the diverse needs of local populations while still adhering to overarching national or international principles. This decentralization can enhance inclusivity, as local authorities are often more attuned to the specifics of their communities compared to a distant central government. In this regard, federalism can be an effective mechanism for promoting equality, as it empowers marginalized groups and facilitates their participation in decision-making processes.

In examining the interplay between federalism and liberalism, it is essential to recognize that these two ideologies can both support and challenge each other. Liberalism emphasizes individual rights and freedoms, advocating for policies that promote social justice and non-discrimination. However, its universalizing tendencies may overlook local contexts and the specific needs of diverse populations. Federalism, on the other hand, inherently recognizes the importance of local governance and can thus provide a platform for enacting liberal values in a manner that is sensitive to regional differences. This symbiotic relationship can foster an environment where equality is not only a theoretical ideal but also a practical reality.

Sovereignty plays a crucial role in shaping inclusive policies within both federal and liberal frameworks. In a globalized world, the challenge lies in balancing the principle of state sovereignty with the need for inclusive policies that address global issues such as migration and human rights. Federal systems often navigate this tension by allowing states or regions to exercise a degree of autonomy while still operating under a unified governance structure. This duality can facilitate the adoption of policies that reflect both local values and broader human rights standards, thereby promoting equality across various spheres of society.

The influence of liberal values on immigration and refugee policies is another critical area where the federal model can have a significant impact. Liberalism advocates for the protection of individual rights, including the rights of migrants and refugees. Federal systems can implement inclusive immigration policies that reflect these liberal principles while also accommodating local concerns. By enabling regions to design their own immigration frameworks, federalism can promote a more equitable approach to migration that balances humanitarian considerations with the realities of local capacity and resources.

The federal model offers a promising avenue for advancing equality in the context of global governance. By harmonizing the principles of liberalism with the practical realities of federal systems, policymakers can create inclusive frameworks that respect the diversity of local communities while adhering to universal human rights standards. As societies continue to grapple with the challenges of inclusion and acceptance, understanding the intersections of federalism, sovereignty, and liberal values will be essential for fostering equitable and cohesive societies.

CASE STUDIES OF FEDERALISM PROMOTING SOCIAL JUSTICE

Case studies of federalism promoting social justice illustrate how decentralized governance can effectively address inequalities and enhance inclusion. One notable example is Canada, where federalism has allowed provinces to implement tailored policies that reflect the diverse needs of their populations. A commitment to social justice is evident in the provincial governments' ability to address issues such as healthcare access, education, and indigenous rights. This localized approach has facilitated the development of programs that are sensitive to cultural and regional differences, thereby fostering an environment where marginalized communities can thrive.

Similarly, the Federal Republic of Germany provides a compelling case of federalism in action, particularly in the realm of social welfare. The Grundgesetz, or Basic Law, emphasizes the importance of human dignity and equality, which is reflected in the decentralized welfare system. Each federal state (Bundesland) has the autonomy to design programs that cater to its unique demographic and economic conditions. This flexibility allows for innovative solutions to social issues, such as homelessness and unemployment, and promotes a sense of local ownership and accountability. Consequently, the federal structure not only empowers local governments but also enhances the efficacy of social justice initiatives.

In contrast, the United States presents a mixed picture of federalism and social justice. While the federal government sets broad civil rights protections, state-level policies often vary significantly, leading to disparities in social outcomes. For instance, states with progressive policies have made strides in areas such as healthcare and education, whereas others have enacted laws that perpetuate inequality. This variability underscores the challenge of reconciling states' rights with the need for consistent social justice frameworks across the nation. Nevertheless, the federal structure allows for experimentation and innovation, as states can serve as laboratories of democracy, testing new approaches to social issues.

Examining the role of federalism in Australia further highlights its potential for promoting social justice. The country's federal system has enabled the implementation of policies aimed at addressing the historical injustices faced by Aboriginal and Torres Strait Islander peoples. Through initiatives like land rights legislation and self-determination policies, federalism has provided a mechanism for indigenous communities to gain greater control over their affairs. This case demonstrates how a federal structure can facilitate the reconciliation process, making room for dialogue and collaboration between governments and marginalized groups, ultimately fostering a more inclusive society.

Finally, Brazil's experience with federalism showcases the complexities of achieving social justice in a diverse society. The Brazilian Constitution establishes a federal system that grants significant powers to states and municipalities, allowing for localized responses to social issues. However, the effectiveness of this system has been challenged by economic disparities and political fragmentation. In urban areas, innovative local governance models have emerged, promoting participatory budgeting and community engagement, which have empowered underrepresented populations. These case studies collectively illustrate that while federalism can serve as a powerful tool for promoting social justice, its success largely depends on the commitment to inclusivity at both the federal and local levels.

The Role *of* Federal Institutions *in* Inclusion

The role of federal institutions in promoting inclusion is critical to understanding how governance structures can effectively address the complexities of diversity in society. Federal institutions, designed to balance power between central and regional authorities, play a key role in implementing policies that foster social cohesion and acceptance. By distributing power and decision-making across various levels of government, federal systems can better respond to the unique needs of diverse populations. This decentralized approach allows for tailored policies that address local concerns while adhering to broader national goals of inclusion and equity.

In the context of global governance, federal institutions can serve as a model for how to integrate liberal values with the need for sovereignty. Liberalism emphasizes individual rights and freedoms, advocating for open societies that embrace diversity. Conversely, federalism provides a framework that respects the autonomy of different regions while promoting inclusive policies. By examining the interaction between these two ideologies, it becomes evident that federal institutions can effectively mediate the potential conflicts between the desire for sovereignty and the imperative of inclusion. They can ensure that inclusive policies are not only formulated but also implemented in ways that resonate with the specific cultural and social contexts of various communities.

Moreover, federal institutions have a significant impact on immigration and refugee policies, areas that are often contentious in discussions of national identity and sovereignty. By allowing regional governments to have a say in immigration policies, federal systems can create more responsive and humane approaches to refugee resettlement and integration. This local involvement can lead to innovative practices that promote social acceptance and economic participation among newcomers, thereby enhancing social cohesion. The effectiveness of such policies is often contingent upon the ability of local governments to engage with their communities and foster a welcoming environment, showcasing the importance of federal structures in addressing these challenges.

Federalism also plays a pivotal role in balancing autonomy and inclusion at the local governance level. Local governments, empowered by federal frameworks, can enact policies that reflect the diversity of their populations. This empowerment promotes a sense of belonging among marginalized groups and can help mitigate feelings of disenfranchisement. When local authorities are equipped to address the specific needs of their communities, they can facilitate a more inclusive society that values every individual's contribution. This balance between local autonomy and overarching federal principles is essential for fostering an environment of acceptance and equality.

The intersection of federalism and liberalism presents a unique opportunity to advance human rights and inclusive policies within the framework of global governance. By navigating the tensions between these ideologies, federal institutions can champion the values of diversity and inclusion while respecting the principles of sovereignty. This dual approach not only enhances domestic social cohesion but also positions nations to engage more effectively in international dialogues about human rights and global cooperation. Through case studies and comparative analyses, it becomes evident that the role of federal institutions is not merely a structural arrangement; it is a vital component of a more inclusive and open society.

THE INTERSECTION OF ECONOMIC POLICIES AND LIBERAL IDEALS IN OPEN SOCIETIES

Economic Liberalism *and* Global Trade

Economic liberalism is a foundational concept in understanding global trade, rooted in the belief that free markets and minimal government intervention stimulate economic growth and foster international cooperation. This perspective advocates for the reduction of trade barriers, which facilitates the flow of goods, services, and capital across borders. By emphasizing the interconnectedness of global economies, economic liberalism posits that nations can achieve mutual benefits through trade agreements and partnerships. This vision aligns with the broader ideals of liberalism, which prioritizes individual freedoms, innovation, and the pursuit of prosperity, creating an environment conducive to open societies.

The interplay between economic liberalism and global trade impacts the discourse surrounding sovereignty and federalism. While economic liberalism encourages states to embrace globalization, it often raises questions about the extent to which national sovereignty can be preserved in the face of global economic forces. Nations may find themselves balancing the need for open markets with the desire to maintain regulatory control over their domestic economies. This tension highlights the ongoing debate within the realms of liberalism and federalism, particularly in how countries can manage their autonomy while participating in an increasingly interconnected world.

In the context of immigration and refugee policies, economic liberalism exerts significant influence. Open trade policies often lead to increased migration as people seek better economic opportunities in more prosperous regions. However, this influx can challenge existing social structures and provoke debates about inclusion and acceptance. Economic liberalism advocates for the free movement of labor, which can enhance cultural diversity and promote social cohesion. Yet, it also necessitates a careful approach to integrating newcomers while respecting the rights and concerns of local populations, underscoring the need for policies that balance economic benefits with social harmony.

Federalism, as a governance framework, offers a potential pathway for addressing the complexities of economic liberalism and global trade. By distributing power between national and local governments, federal systems can create tailored approaches to economic policy that reflect regional needs and priorities. This decentralization allows for more nuanced responses to the challenges posed by globalization, fostering inclusion and acceptance at local levels. Moreover, federalism can facilitate cooperation among diverse groups, promoting equality and ensuring that the voices of various communities are heard in the economic decision-making process.

The relationship between economic liberalism and global trade is multifaceted and deeply intertwined with issues of sovereignty, inclusion, and human rights. As societies navigate the challenges of globalization, the principles of liberalism must be reconciled with the realities of federal governance. This dynamic interplay shapes the policies that govern trade, immigration, and social cohesion, influencing how nations approach their commitments to both economic growth and inclusive societies. By examining these themes, we can better understand the complexities of fostering an open world that embraces diversity while promoting shared prosperity.

The Impact *of* Economic Policies *on* Inclusion

Economic policies play a crucial role in shaping the landscape of inclusion within societies, particularly in the context of open societies that strive for equality and acceptance. These policies can either facilitate or hinder the integration of marginalized groups, influencing their access to resources, opportunities, and social recognition. In liberal democracies, economic frameworks often emphasize individual rights and market-driven solutions, which can lead to disparities if not paired with robust mechanisms aimed at inclusion. Conversely, federal systems, with their decentralized governance structures, can adapt policies to meet the specific needs of diverse communities, potentially enhancing inclusion and social cohesion.

The impact of economic policies on inclusion is particularly pronounced in immigration and refugee contexts. Liberal values traditionally advocate for open borders and the humane treatment of displaced individuals, often resulting in policies that prioritize human rights. However, the economic implications of such policies can lead to tensions. For instance, while welcoming immigrants may enhance cultural diversity, it can also strain local economies and public services if not managed effectively. On the other hand, federal systems can implement tailored economic policies that address the concerns of local populations, promoting both economic stability and social inclusion by engaging communities in decision-making processes.

Federalism, with its emphasis on local governance, presents a unique opportunity to balance autonomy and inclusion. Local governments are often more attuned to the specific needs of their communities, allowing for economic policies that reflect local conditions and values. This localized approach can foster inclusivity by ensuring that marginalized voices are heard in the policymaking process. By engaging communities in developing economic initiatives, federal systems can create pathways for participation and representation, ultimately enhancing social cohesion and reducing economic disparities.

Economic policies also intersect with the broader themes of human rights and sovereignty. In an increasingly globalized world, the tension between national sovereignty and the need for inclusive policies becomes apparent. While states may seek to maintain control over their economic strategies, the pursuit of inclusive policies often requires cooperation beyond borders. Liberalism advocates for a global approach to human rights, encouraging economic policies that transcend national boundaries. This creates a complex dynamic where states must navigate their sovereignty while striving to implement policies that promote equality and acceptance for all individuals, regardless of their background.

In conclusion, the relationship between economic policies and inclusion is multifaceted and deeply influenced by the ideological lenses of liberalism and federalism. Both frameworks offer valuable insights into how societies can structure their economic policies to promote inclusion and acceptance. While liberalism emphasizes individual rights and humanitarian principles, federalism allows for localized approaches that can better address the unique challenges faced by diverse communities. Understanding this interplay is essential for developing economic strategies that not only drive growth but also foster an open and inclusive society.

CASE STUDIES OF ECONOMIC DISPARITIES AND SOCIAL INCLUSION

Economic disparities have become a focal point in discussions about social inclusion, particularly as societies grapple with the challenges posed by globalization and the quest for equitable policies. Case studies across various nations provide valuable insights into how economic inequalities affect the integration of diverse groups within communities. For instance, examining the economic policies in Scandinavian countries reveals a commitment to social welfare that has facilitated greater inclusion of marginalized groups, contributing to both social cohesion and economic stability. These nations illustrate how proactive measures can bridge economic gaps, ensuring that all citizens benefit from national prosperity.

In contrast, the United States presents a more complex picture of economic disparity and social inclusion. The widening income gap and the varying access to resources among different racial and ethnic groups highlight the challenges that arise in a system that often prioritizes individualism over collective welfare. Case studies from urban centers like New York City and Chicago show how federal policies can either exacerbate or alleviate these disparities. While programs aimed at improving education and employment opportunities have shown some success, the underlying structural inequalities remain a significant barrier to comprehensive social inclusion.

Canada offers a different approach, with a federal system that emphasizes multiculturalism and social inclusion through its policies. The country's immigration framework is designed to attract diverse populations while promoting economic participation. Case studies from cities such as Toronto illustrate how federal support for local initiatives can enhance social integration, allowing various communities to thrive economically and socially. This demonstrates that a federalist approach, when paired with inclusive policies, can effectively address economic disparities and foster a sense of belonging among diverse populations.

The intersection of economic policies and liberal ideals is also evident in the European Union, where member states strive for both economic growth and social inclusion. Case studies from countries like Germany and Sweden highlight the impact of liberal values on immigration and refugee policies, showcasing how these nations balance the dual goals of economic productivity and social responsibility. By investing in programs that support immigrant integration, these countries not only promote diversity but also leverage it as a driver for economic innovation and growth.

Ultimately, the exploration of case studies on economic disparities and social inclusion reveals that both liberalism and federalism can play crucial roles in shaping inclusive policies. While challenges persist, particularly in contexts where sovereignty and national interests may conflict with global obligations, the examples set by various countries illustrate that thoughtful governance can create pathways for economic equity. These case studies emphasize the importance of collaborative approaches that integrate economic and social policies, ensuring that all individuals have the opportunity to contribute to and benefit from an open society.

HISTORICAL PERSPECTIVES ON FEDERALISM SOVEREIGNTY AND LIBERAL THOUGHT

Evolution *of* Federalist Thought

The evolution of federalist thought has played a significant role in shaping contemporary political discourse, particularly in the context of sovereignty and global governance. Emerging from the backdrop of Enlightenment ideas, federalism originally sought to balance the need for a centralized authority with the preservation of local autonomy. This duality reflects an ongoing tension in political philosophy: how to foster unity and effective governance while respecting the unique identities and rights of diverse communities. The historical roots of federalism can be traced back to early attempts at confederation, where the emphasis was placed on cooperative governance structures that could accommodate various interests and promote collective well-being.

As federalist thought matured, it began to engage more directly with the principles of liberalism. Advocates of federalism recognized that an inclusive society requires not only a framework for governance but also a commitment to individual rights and freedoms. This intersection has been particularly evident in debates surrounding immigration and refugee policies, where the challenge lies in balancing national sovereignty with the imperative to uphold human rights. By examining case studies that highlight the practical applications of federalist principles, one can discern how these frameworks have facilitated both the inclusion of marginalized groups and the maintenance of social cohesion within diverse populations.

The role of sovereignty in promoting inclusive policies is also a critical component of federalist thought. While traditional notions of sovereignty often emphasize territorial integrity and national self-determination, modern interpretations increasingly recognize the necessity of engaging with global governance structures. This shift reflects a growing understanding that national borders cannot fully encapsulate the realities of migration and multiculturalism. Federalist perspectives advocate for a reimagined sovereignty that is flexible enough to accommodate international norms while still protecting local interests, ultimately fostering an environment where diversity is celebrated rather than merely tolerated.

Federalism's inherent adaptability positions it as a viable framework for promoting equality and acceptance in an increasingly interconnected world. By enabling local governance, federal systems can tailor policies that reflect the specific needs and aspirations of their communities. This localized approach not only empowers citizens but also ensures that diverse voices are represented in the decision-making process. The interplay between federalism and local governance has the potential to bridge divides, allowing for the development of inclusive policies that address the unique challenges faced by various groups within a society.

The evolution of federalist thought offers valuable insights into the ongoing dialogue between liberalism and sovereignty. As global challenges intensify, the quest for an open society that embraces inclusivity and acceptance becomes ever more pressing. By examining the historical trajectories and contemporary applications of federalist principles, one can better understand their relevance in promoting human rights, fostering social cohesion, and navigating the complexities of global governance. This comparative analysis not only highlights the strengths and weaknesses of both liberal and federalist ideologies but also underscores the importance of integrating diverse perspectives in the pursuit of a more equitable and harmonious world.

Historical Context *of* Sovereignty

The concept of sovereignty has evolved significantly throughout history, shaped by philosophical, political, and social developments. In the early modern period, the Treaty of Westphalia (1648) marked a pivotal moment, establishing the principle of state sovereignty as a cornerstone of international relations. This treaty concluded the Thirty Years' War in Europe and recognized the rights of states to govern themselves without external interference. The Westphalian model effectively laid the groundwork for the modern nation-state system, emphasizing territorial integrity and the authority of governments over their populations. This historical context is crucial for understanding contemporary debates surrounding sovereignty, particularly in the light of globalization and the increasing importance of transnational governance structures.

Liberalism emerged as a powerful ideological force in the Enlightenment era, advocating for individual rights, democracy, and the rule of law. This philosophy championed the idea that sovereignty should be exercised in ways that promote the welfare and freedoms of individuals. As liberal thought gained traction, it began to challenge traditional notions of absolute sovereignty, arguing for a framework that includes human rights and social justice. The tension between liberal ideals and the concept of state sovereignty became evident, especially as liberalism called for greater inclusion and acceptance of diverse populations within nation-states. This dialectic continues to inform contemporary discussions on how sovereignty can coexist with the need for open societies that embrace multiculturalism.

Federalism, by contrast, offers a different perspective on governance and sovereignty. It emphasizes the distribution of power across multiple levels of government, allowing for a balance between national authority and local autonomy. Historical examples of federalism, such as the United States and Switzerland, illustrate how this system can foster inclusive policies that reflect the diverse needs of various communities. Federalism can serve as a mechanism for promoting equality and acceptance by ensuring that local voices are heard and represented in the decision-making process. In this context, sovereignty is not merely about the power of the state but is redefined to incorporate a commitment to inclusivity and the protection of minority rights.

The intersection of liberal values and federalism raises important questions about immigration and refugee policies. Liberalism's emphasis on human rights and humanitarian values often advocates for open borders and the inclusion of displaced persons. However, the challenge lies in reconciling these ideals with the sovereignty of states, which may seek to control their borders and regulate immigration based on national interest. The federalist approach may offer solutions by allowing local governments to tailor policies that reflect the unique contexts and demographics of their regions. This dual approach can promote both the protection of individual rights and the integrity of sovereign states, ultimately facilitating a more inclusive global governance framework.

In analyzing the historical context of sovereignty, it is essential to recognize the ongoing tensions between liberalism and federalism. Both frameworks offer valuable insights into how societies can navigate the complexities of global governance while striving for inclusivity and acceptance. As the world becomes increasingly interconnected, the need for innovative approaches that balance sovereign rights with the imperatives of an open society is more critical than ever. Understanding these historical perspectives not only informs current debates but also provides a foundation for envisioning a future where sovereignty can coexist harmoniously with the aspirations for a more inclusive and equitable world.

Liberalism's Historical Roots *and* Development

Liberalism, as a political and philosophical doctrine, has deep historical roots that trace back to the Enlightenment era in Europe, where thinkers like John Locke, Jean-Jacques Rousseau, and Voltaire laid the groundwork for modern democratic ideals. Central to liberal thought is the belief in individual rights, personal freedoms, and the importance of reasoned discourse in governance. This intellectual movement emerged in response to the absolutist monarchies and feudal systems that characterized earlier European societies, advocating for a system of governance that prioritizes the individual over the state. The evolution of liberalism during this period was crucial in shaping concepts of citizenship, participation, and the rule of law, which would later influence global governance frameworks.

As liberalism developed, it began to intersect with the rise of nationalism and the formation of modern states, leading to a complex relationship with sovereignty. The transition from feudal allegiances to nation-states meant that the liberal emphasis on individual rights had to be reconciled with the necessity of a cohesive national identity and governance structure. This reconciliation was not without tension, as the expansion of liberal democracy often clashed with the demands for sovereignty, particularly in post-colonial contexts where newly independent nations sought to forge their paths. The historical trajectory of liberalism thus reflects an ongoing negotiation between the ideals of openness and inclusion and the realities of state sovereignty and national interests.

In contemporary discourse, the principles of liberalism have significantly influenced immigration and refugee policies across the globe. Many liberal democracies have embraced the idea that welcoming diverse populations enhances societal richness and contributes to economic vitality. However, this approach also faces challenges as states grapple with balancing liberal ideals of inclusion with concerns over national security, social cohesion, and the welfare of existing citizens. The historical context of liberal thought provides a framework for understanding these tensions, as it highlights the need for policies that not only recognize the rights of newcomers but also ensure that existing community values and resources are not undermined.

The relationship between federalism and liberalism offers a unique perspective on governance that seeks to balance autonomy with inclusivity. Federal systems allow for the decentralization of power, enabling local governments to address the specific needs of their communities while adhering to broader national or supranational principles. This approach can promote equality and acceptance by ensuring that diverse voices are heard and represented in governance structures. However, the effectiveness of federalism in promoting inclusivity often depends on the underlying liberal framework that supports individual rights and communal harmony, making the historical interplay between these concepts essential for understanding current governance challenges.

The evolution of liberalism and its interaction with federalism and sovereignty continues to shape contemporary global governance. As societies navigate complex issues such as human rights, economic policies, and multiculturalism, the historical roots of liberal thought provide a vital lens through which to examine these dynamics. Case studies of liberalism and federalism in action illustrate the potential for collaboration and conflict in promoting global peace and cooperation. Ultimately, the historical development of liberalism not only informs our understanding of past governance models but also serves as a guide for addressing the dilemmas of inclusion and acceptance in an increasingly interconnected world.

CASE STUDIES OF LIBERALISM AND FEDERALISM IN PROMOTING GLOBAL PEACE AND COOPERATION

Successful Liberal *and* Federalist Models

Liberalism and federalism present frameworks that can successfully navigate the complexities of sovereignty and inclusion in global governance. Liberalism emphasizes individual rights, freedoms, and equality, advocating for policies that promote open societies and multiculturalism. This ideological approach fosters an environment where diversity is not only accepted but celebrated, encouraging nations to adopt inclusive immigration and refugee policies. The liberal model promotes human rights as a universal standard, asserting that respecting these rights is essential for maintaining social cohesion and fostering democratic values. As countries strive to create inclusive societies, the liberal approach serves as a guiding principle for developing policies that prioritize human dignity and equality.

In contrast, federalism offers a unique structure for governance that balances local autonomy with broader national or international objectives. By distributing power among various levels of government, federalism allows for regional diversity while ensuring that local voices are heard in the decision-making process. This model is particularly beneficial in multi-ethnic societies, where different cultural groups may seek a degree of self-governance. Successful federalist models can promote inclusion by providing mechanisms for minority representation and participation. This decentralization of power can lead to more localized policies that reflect the needs and aspirations of diverse communities, thus enhancing social acceptance and reducing tensions.

The role of sovereignty in these models is crucial, as it directly impacts the effectiveness of inclusive policies. Sovereignty, often viewed as a barrier to international cooperation, can also be a facilitator of inclusive governance when aligned with liberal and federalist principles. States that embrace sovereignty while committing to human rights and inclusion can create policies that not only protect their citizens but also promote global cooperation. By recognizing that sovereignty does not preclude collaboration, nations can work together to address transnational issues such as migration, climate change, and human rights violations, fostering a more interconnected and supportive global community.

The intersection of economic policies with liberal ideals further illustrates the potential for successful governance models. Economic liberalism advocates for free markets and open trade, which can enhance global connectivity and promote equality. Federalism complements this by allowing for regional economic policies that cater to local needs while contributing to national economic goals. By ensuring that economic opportunities are accessible to all segments of society, both models can promote social cohesion and reduce disparities. This economic inclusivity can enhance the overall stability of societies, leading to more peaceful and cooperative international relations.

Historical perspectives on the interplay between federalism, sovereignty, and liberal thought reveal that successful governance often arises from a synthesis of these models. Case studies demonstrate that nations that blend liberal values with federalist structures can effectively manage diversity and promote stability. By analyzing past successes and challenges, contemporary policymakers can glean insights into how to construct inclusive governance frameworks that respect both individual rights and collective autonomy. Such an approach not only addresses the immediate needs of diverse populations but also contributes to long-term global peace and cooperation, setting the stage for a more open and accepting world.

Lessons *from* International Cooperation Initiatives

International cooperation initiatives provide a rich landscape for examining the interplay between liberalism, federalism, and sovereignty. These initiatives often reveal the complexities involved in balancing national interests with global imperatives. As nations come together to address pressing issues such as climate change, health crises, and economic disparities, the lessons drawn from their collaborative efforts highlight both the potential and the limitations inherent in various governance models. Observing how different countries navigate these challenges can inform broader discussions on the efficacy of liberal and federalist approaches in promoting inclusive policies.

One key lesson from international cooperation is the necessity of fostering open dialogue among diverse stakeholders. In many successful initiatives, the inclusion of various voices—ranging from governments to civil society organizations—has been fundamental in achieving consensus. This inclusive approach aligns with liberal principles that advocate for participation and representation. However, it also raises questions about the degree to which federal structures can facilitate such dialogues while respecting the sovereignty of individual states. The tension between local governance and international commitments often necessitates innovative solutions that honor both autonomy and cooperation.

Moreover, the impact of liberal values on immigration and refugee policies is a critical area where international cooperation has proven essential. Countries that embrace liberal ideals tend to prioritize human rights and humanitarian assistance, leading to more welcoming policies for migrants and refugees. However, the challenge remains in reconciling these liberal values with the sovereignty concerns that drive some nations to adopt more restrictive measures. Examining case studies of countries that have successfully balanced these competing priorities can provide valuable insights into how federalism can serve as a framework for promoting equality and acceptance in the face of global migration trends.

The role of economic policies in shaping the dynamics of international cooperation cannot be overlooked. Liberal ideals often emphasize free markets and economic integration, which can enhance cooperation and mutual benefit among nations. However, federalism introduces a layer of complexity by necessitating local governance structures that can both support and challenge these liberal economic frameworks. The intersection of economic policies and governance models highlights the need for a nuanced understanding of how to create inclusive economic opportunities while respecting the unique contexts of different regions and communities.

Finally, the historical perspectives on federalism, sovereignty, and liberal thought offer critical insights into contemporary challenges in global governance. By analyzing past international cooperation initiatives, it becomes evident that the lessons learned are not merely academic but have tangible implications for current policy-making. The interplay of human rights, sovereignty, and social cohesion within these historical contexts can guide modern efforts to navigate the tensions that arise in global affairs. As nations continue to grapple with issues of inclusion and acceptance, the experiences derived from these initiatives will be invaluable in shaping a more cohesive and equitable global community.

Recommendations *for* Future Global Governance

In considering the future of global governance, it is essential to integrate the principles of liberalism and federalism to create a more inclusive and equitable system. The interplay between these two ideologies presents a unique opportunity to address pressing global challenges while respecting the sovereignty of nations. Recommendations should focus on fostering collaborative frameworks that prioritize human rights and social cohesion, enabling states to work together without compromising their autonomy. By emphasizing the shared values of inclusion and acceptance, global governance can evolve into a more effective mechanism for addressing the diverse needs of populations worldwide.

One key recommendation is to establish international institutions that reflect the ideals of both liberalism and federalism. These institutions should facilitate dialogue among nations and promote policies that enhance inclusivity while respecting sovereignty. By creating platforms for cooperation, countries can share best practices regarding immigration and refugee policies, which are critical in an increasingly mobile world. This collaborative approach can help mitigate tensions arising from differing national interests while promoting a cohesive global strategy that prioritizes human dignity and rights.

Furthermore, a renewed focus on local governance within a federal framework can empower communities to address their unique challenges while contributing to national and global objectives. Such a model allows for the balancing of autonomy and inclusion, ensuring that local voices are heard in the decision-making process. By investing in local capacities and promoting participatory governance, states can foster a sense of ownership among citizens, leading to more effective implementation of inclusive policies. This approach not only enhances social cohesion but also strengthens the legitimacy of governmental actions at all levels.

Education plays a crucial role in shaping public perceptions of liberalism and federalism, particularly regarding multiculturalism and social acceptance. Future global governance should prioritize educational initiatives that promote understanding and respect among diverse cultures. By fostering a global citizenry that values inclusion and equality, societies can better navigate the complexities of immigration and refugee issues. Education can serve as a powerful tool to counteract prejudice and encourage acceptance, ultimately contributing to a more peaceful and cooperative international environment.

Finally, the intersection of economic policies and liberal ideals must be carefully managed to ensure that the benefits of globalization are equitably distributed. Future recommendations for global governance should include frameworks that promote economic equality while respecting the principles of sovereignty. By aligning economic strategies with inclusive policies, countries can work towards reducing disparities that often lead to social unrest. A commitment to fair trade, sustainable development, and equitable resource distribution will be essential in creating a more just global society, where the ideals of liberalism and federalism can thrive together.

NAVIGATING THE OPEN SOCIETY DILEMMA

The analysis presented in this book reveals a complex interplay between liberalism, federalism, and sovereignty, particularly in the context of global governance. A central finding is that while liberalism advocates for open societies characterized by inclusion and acceptance, it often clashes with the principle of sovereignty, which can sometimes hinder the realization of these ideals. The desire for an open world is frequently compromised by national interests that prioritize state autonomy over global cooperation. This tension underscores the necessity for a nuanced understanding of how these frameworks interact and affect policy-making on both local and global levels.

A comparative analysis of liberalism and federalism showcases their differing approaches to governance and inclusion. Liberalism tends to emphasize individual rights and freedoms, advocating for policies that promote multiculturalism and social cohesion. In contrast, federalism offers a structural approach that allows for the distribution of power among various levels of government, which can enhance local governance while still fostering inclusive policies. This divergence points to the potential for federalism to serve as a bridge between the ideals of liberalism and the realities of sovereignty, suggesting that a hybrid model may be beneficial for addressing contemporary global challenges.

The role of sovereignty in promoting inclusive policies has emerged as a critical theme. While sovereignty is often viewed as a barrier to inclusive practices, this study highlights examples where sovereign states have successfully implemented policies that align with liberal values. These instances reveal that when states prioritize human rights within the framework of their sovereignty, they can create environments that support both national interests and global inclusivity. This balance is essential for navigating the complexities of international relations, particularly in the context of immigration and refugee policies that are heavily influenced by liberal ideals.

The findings also underscore the impact of liberal values on immigration and refugee policies, illustrating how these values shape public discourse and legislative frameworks. Countries that embrace liberal principles tend to adopt more welcoming stances towards immigrants and refugees, fostering environments conducive to diversity and multiculturalism. However, this is often challenged by rising nationalism and resistance to immigration, which complicates the pursuit of inclusive policies. The book suggests that understanding these dynamics is crucial for developing effective strategies that reconcile liberal ideals with the realities of public sentiment.

The intersection of economic policies with liberal ideals in open societies reveals another layer of complexity in the discussion of sovereignty and inclusion. Economic frameworks that prioritize equality and acceptance can reinforce liberal values and promote social cohesion. However, the pursuit of economic growth can sometimes lead to exclusionary practices that undermine these very principles. The historical perspectives provided in the book illustrate how federalism has historically adapted to these challenges, offering a potential path forward in the quest for global peace and cooperation. By analyzing key case studies, the findings advocate for a balanced approach that leverages the strengths of both liberalism and federalism to foster a more inclusive and equitable global society.

Future Directions *for* Research and Policy

As the discourse surrounding global governance continues to evolve, future research must prioritize a nuanced understanding of the interplay between liberalism and federalism. This includes examining how these ideologies can coalesce to address pressing global issues such as migration, climate change, and inequality. Scholars should investigate models that integrate both frameworks, exploring how liberal values can coexist with federal structures to promote inclusive policies. A comparative analysis across different contexts will be essential to identify successful practices and frameworks that can be adapted for broader application.

In addition to theoretical explorations, empirical studies are needed to assess the impact of sovereignty on inclusive policies.

Researchers should delve into case studies that illustrate how sovereign states can implement policies that uphold human rights while respecting the need for local governance and autonomy. The tension between national sovereignty and global humanitarian obligations presents a critical area for inquiry. Understanding how states navigate this tension can provide valuable insights for policymakers aiming to create frameworks that foster both security and inclusivity.

The role of liberal values in shaping immigration and refugee policies demands further attention. It is essential to analyze how liberal principles can inform equitable and humane immigration practices while balancing national interests. Future research should explore the consequences of liberal immigration policies on social cohesion and multiculturalism, assessing both the successes and challenges faced by nations that have embraced these values. This analysis can guide policymakers in developing comprehensive immigration strategies that align with liberal ideals while addressing public concerns.

Moreover, the relationship between federalism and local governance deserves a more profound investigation, particularly concerning autonomy and inclusion. Future studies should examine how federal systems can effectively balance the need for local self-governance with the overarching goals of national unity and inclusivity. This research will be critical for understanding how federal structures can adapt to diverse social landscapes, promoting equality and acceptance across different communities. By focusing on the dynamics of local governance within federal systems, scholars can contribute to a more comprehensive understanding of how to achieve inclusive governance.

Finally, the intersection of economic policies and liberal ideals presents a fertile ground for future research. Investigating how economic strategies can reflect and promote liberal values of equality and acceptance will be crucial in an increasingly interconnected world. Researchers should analyze case studies of nations that have successfully aligned their economic policies with liberal principles, as well as those that have encountered challenges. These insights can inform policymakers on designing economic frameworks that not only stimulate growth but also foster social cohesion and inclusivity, ultimately contributing to the realization of the open society ideal.

The Path Forward *for* Open Societies

The path forward for open societies necessitates a nuanced understanding of the interplay between liberalism, federalism, and sovereignty. As nations grapple with the complexities of globalization, it becomes increasingly vital to recognize how these frameworks can coexist to promote inclusivity and acceptance. Liberalism, with its emphasis on individual rights and freedoms, offers a compelling vision for an open world. However, without the balancing act of federalism, which promotes local governance and autonomy, the implementation of these ideals can be uneven, potentially leading to societal fragmentation. A comparative analysis of both frameworks reveals that a harmonious integration of liberal principles with federalist structures may provide the most promising avenue for fostering an inclusive global community.

In addressing the role of sovereignty in promoting inclusive policies, it is essential to acknowledge that sovereignty does not inherently conflict with the ideals of openness. Instead, sovereignty can serve as a protective mechanism that empowers nations to adopt policies that reflect their unique cultural and social contexts while still engaging in global dialogue. By embracing a model of sovereignty that prioritizes human rights and inclusive governance, states can navigate the complexities of global interdependence without sacrificing their autonomy. This approach emphasizes that while states are sovereign entities, their responsibilities extend beyond borders, necessitating cooperation in addressing challenges such as migration, climate change, and social inequality.

The impact of liberal values on immigration and refugee policies further illustrates the dynamic tension between liberalism and federalism. Liberal societies often champion the rights of immigrants and refugees, viewing them as integral to their multicultural fabric. However, the desire for acceptance must be matched by appropriate regulatory frameworks that local governments can enforce. Federalism allows for tailored responses to immigration challenges, enabling regions to adopt policies that reflect their capacities and social contexts. By fostering local governance that aligns with liberal principles, open societies can create environments that both welcome newcomers and enhance social cohesion.

Federalism, as a framework for promoting equality and acceptance, presents opportunities for local communities to engage in policymaking that reflects diverse perspectives. The decentralized nature of federalism facilitates dialogue among various cultural groups, allowing for the development of policies that genuinely embody the principles of inclusion. Moreover, federalist structures can mitigate the risks of cultural homogenization by empowering minority voices and ensuring their representation in decision-making processes. This balance between autonomy and inclusivity is crucial in building resilient societies that can withstand the pressures of globalization while remaining committed to the ideals of open societies.

Finally, the intersection of economic policies and liberal ideals cannot be overlooked in the pursuit of open societies. Economic frameworks that prioritize inclusivity and equality are essential for fostering social cohesion and stability. Liberalism advocates for free markets and individual entrepreneurship, but these must be complemented by federalist approaches that ensure equitable resource distribution and support for marginalized communities. Case studies across various nations demonstrate that integrating liberal economic policies with federalist governance structures can lead to more sustainable and inclusive outcomes. In conclusion, the path forward for open societies lies in the delicate balance of liberalism and federalism, guided by a commitment to sovereignty that embraces inclusivity and promotes global cooperation.

THE KALEIDOSCOPE OF POWER
FINAL CONSIDERATIONS

NAVIGATING THE MULTIFACETED EVOLUTION OF POLITICAL SYSTEMS FOR A FUTURE OF INCLUSIVITY

The political landscapes of the EU and the US are intricate, involving federalization, decentralization, populism, sovereignty, and liberalism. These forces, often contradictory and always evolving, shape the contours of governance, influence societal structures, and ultimately determine the quality of human experience. Understanding these doctrines not merely as abstract concepts, but as powerful engines driving societal change, is crucial if we hope to build a future defined by inclusivity, diversity, acceptance, and love — a world where human potential flourishes unburdened by the shackles of prejudice and inequity.

The journey towards understanding this complex interplay begins with acknowledging the multifaceted nature of evolution. Political systems are not static entities. They respond to internal pressures, external influences, and the evolving needs of their citizens. In the EU, the pendulum swings between greater federalization, exemplified by the establishment of common institutions and policies, and decentralization, fueled by regionalism and nationalistic sentiment seeking to reclaim sovereignty. The US, too, grapples with this tension, witnessed in the ongoing debates surrounding states' rights and the role of the federal government. Historically, both systems have demonstrated the benefits and drawbacks of each approach. Federalization can foster economic integration, standardize regulations, and facilitate collective action on global challenges like climate change. However, it can also lead to bureaucratic inefficiencies, a disconnect from local needs, and the erosion of national identities. Decentralization, conversely, empowers local communities, fosters innovation tailored to specific contexts, and strengthens democratic participation. Yet, it can also exacerbate regional inequalities, hinder coordinated responses to crises, and fuel protectionist sentiments.

The rise of populism in both the EU and the US further complicates this dynamic. Often presented as a rebellion against established elites and a championing of the "common person," populism exploits existing anxieties and frustrations, often simplifying complex issues and resorting to divisive rhetoric. While it can serve as a corrective mechanism, holding power accountable and amplifying marginalized voices, it also carries the risk of undermining democratic institutions, promoting exclusionary nationalism, and eroding trust in established norms. Brexit, the rise of nationalist parties across Europe, and the Trump presidency in the US serve as stark reminders of the power and potential dangers of populism.

The concept of sovereignty, traditionally defined as the supreme authority within a territory, is also undergoing profound shifts. In the EU, the sharing of sovereignty through membership in the Union has brought tangible benefits, including economic prosperity and increased international influence. However, it has also been met with resistance, particularly from those who perceive it as a loss of national control and cultural identity. Similarly, in the US, the debate over the limits of federal power often revolves around questions of state sovereignty and individual liberty. The challenge lies in finding a balance between national unity and regional autonomy, ensuring that sovereignty serves the interests of all citizens while respecting their diverse needs and aspirations.

Liberalism, with its emphasis on individual rights, freedoms, and democratic governance, has historically been a cornerstone of both the EU and the US. However, in recent years, liberalism has come under attack from various quarters. Critics on the left argue that it has failed to address systemic inequalities and has been coopted by corporate interests. Critics on the right contend that it has eroded traditional values and promoted cultural relativism. Despite these criticisms, the core principles of liberalism – including the rule of law, freedom of expression, and equal opportunity – remain essential for creating a just and equitable society.

Understanding the interplay of these doctrines is paramount for building a better future. We must move beyond simplistic dichotomies and embrace nuanced perspectives that acknowledge the complexities of human society. This requires:

- **Critical thinking and media literacy:** To navigate the information age, we need to cultivate critical thinking skills and develop the ability to distinguish between credible sources and propaganda.

- **Empathy and intercultural understanding:** Building a future of inclusivity requires us to understand and appreciate different cultures, perspectives, and experiences.

- **Civic engagement and democratic participation:** Active participation in democratic processes is essential for holding power accountable and shaping policies that reflect the needs of all citizens.

- **Education focused on critical analysis and ethical reasoning:** Our educational systems must equip future generations with the skills necessary to navigate the complexities of the 21st century and to make informed decisions based on ethical principles.

- **A commitment to social justice and equality:** We must actively work to dismantle systems of oppression and discrimination and to create a society where everyone has the opportunity to thrive.

Ultimately, the future we create will depend on our ability to learn from the past, understand the present, and envision a better future. By engaging with the multifaceted evolutions of political systems in the EU and the US, by critically examining the implications of federalization, decentralization, populism, sovereignty, and liberalism, we can equip ourselves with the knowledge and tools necessary to build a world characterized by inclusivity, diversity, acceptance, love, and a shared commitment to the well-being of all humanity. This is not merely a political project, but a moral imperative, a call to action to shape a future where the kaleidoscope of power reflects the beauty and richness of the human experience.

BRIDGING THE ATLANTIC

A FUTURE FORGED IN UNDERSTANDING AND EMPATHY

As we conclude our exploration of political systems in the European Union and the United States, it is evident that this journey goes beyond mere retrospective analysis. It is a call to action, a philosophical imperative to understand the complex interplay of doctrines and their impact on society, so that we may actively construct a better future, one defined by inclusivity, diversity, acceptance, and, ultimately, love.

Throughout these pages, we have examined the divergent paths taken by the EU and the US, charting their responses to crises, their internal power struggles, and the shifting sands of global politics. We have dissected the nuanced tapestry of American federalism, the enduring influence of its revolutionary ideals, and the persistent tension between individual liberty and collective security. Simultaneously, we have navigated the intricate architecture of the EU, a supranational entity born from the ashes of war, striving for unity amidst a symphony of national identities and competing interests.

These explorations reveal a crucial truth: political systems are not static entities. They are living organisms, constantly evolving in response to internal and external pressures, adapting to new challenges, and often, succumbing to inherent contradictions. Understanding these evolutionary processes is paramount, not merely for academics and policymakers, but for every citizen who seeks to participate meaningfully in shaping their own destiny.

The doctrines that underpin these systems – liberalism, conservatism, socialism, and the myriad variations thereof – are not abstract concepts confined to textbooks. They are powerful forces that shape our laws, our social norms, and our very perceptions of the world. To ignore them is to be at the mercy of their influence, vulnerable to manipulation and susceptible to the perpetuation of injustice. Only through critical examination can we discern their strengths and weaknesses, their promises and pitfalls.

And here lies the crux of our philosophical endeavor. The ultimate goal of understanding political systems transcends mere intellectual curiosity. It is a moral imperative, driven by the desire to create a more just and equitable world. A world where inclusivity is not just a buzzword but a lived reality, where diversity is celebrated as a strength and not feared as a threat, where acceptance replaces judgment, and where love, in its broadest and most compassionate sense, guides our interactions with one another.

This vision requires a profound shift in perspective. We must move beyond the tribalism that often characterizes political discourse, the "us versus them" mentality that fuels division and obstructs progress. We must cultivate empathy, the ability to understand and share the feelings of others, even those whose beliefs and experiences differ from our own. We must embrace dialogue, engaging in open and honest conversations, listening attentively, and seeking common ground, even when disagreements persist.

The transatlantic relationship, despite its historical complexities and ongoing challenges, offers a powerful model for such dialogue. By learning from each other's successes and failures, by acknowledging our shared values and addressing our divergent approaches, the EU and the US can become catalysts for positive change on a global scale. This requires a commitment to multilateralism, a willingness to collaborate on issues of common concern, and a rejection of isolationist tendencies.

Building a better future necessitates a critical examination of the historical injustices that continue to plague our societies. The legacies of slavery, colonialism, and discrimination continue to shape our present, perpetuating inequalities and undermining social cohesion. Addressing these legacies requires more than just apologies and symbolic gestures. It demands concrete action to dismantle systemic barriers, to ensure equal opportunity for all, and to actively promote reconciliation and healing.

Finally, and perhaps most importantly, we must cultivate a sense of shared humanity. In an increasingly interconnected world, where the challenges we face – climate change, pandemics, economic inequality – transcend national borders, we must recognize that we are all members of a global community. Our fates are intertwined, and our collective survival depends on our ability to cooperate and collaborate.

Bridging the Atlantic is not simply a matter of geographical proximity or political alliance. It is a philosophical endeavor, a commitment to understanding, empathy, and action. By embracing the lessons learned from the evolution of political systems in the EU and the US, by critically examining the doctrines that shape our world, and by cultivating a sense of shared humanity, we can forge a future defined by inclusivity, diversity, acceptance, and love. This is the challenge that lies before us, and it is one that we must embrace with courage, conviction, and unwavering hope. Only then can we truly shape a better world for ourselves and for generations to come.

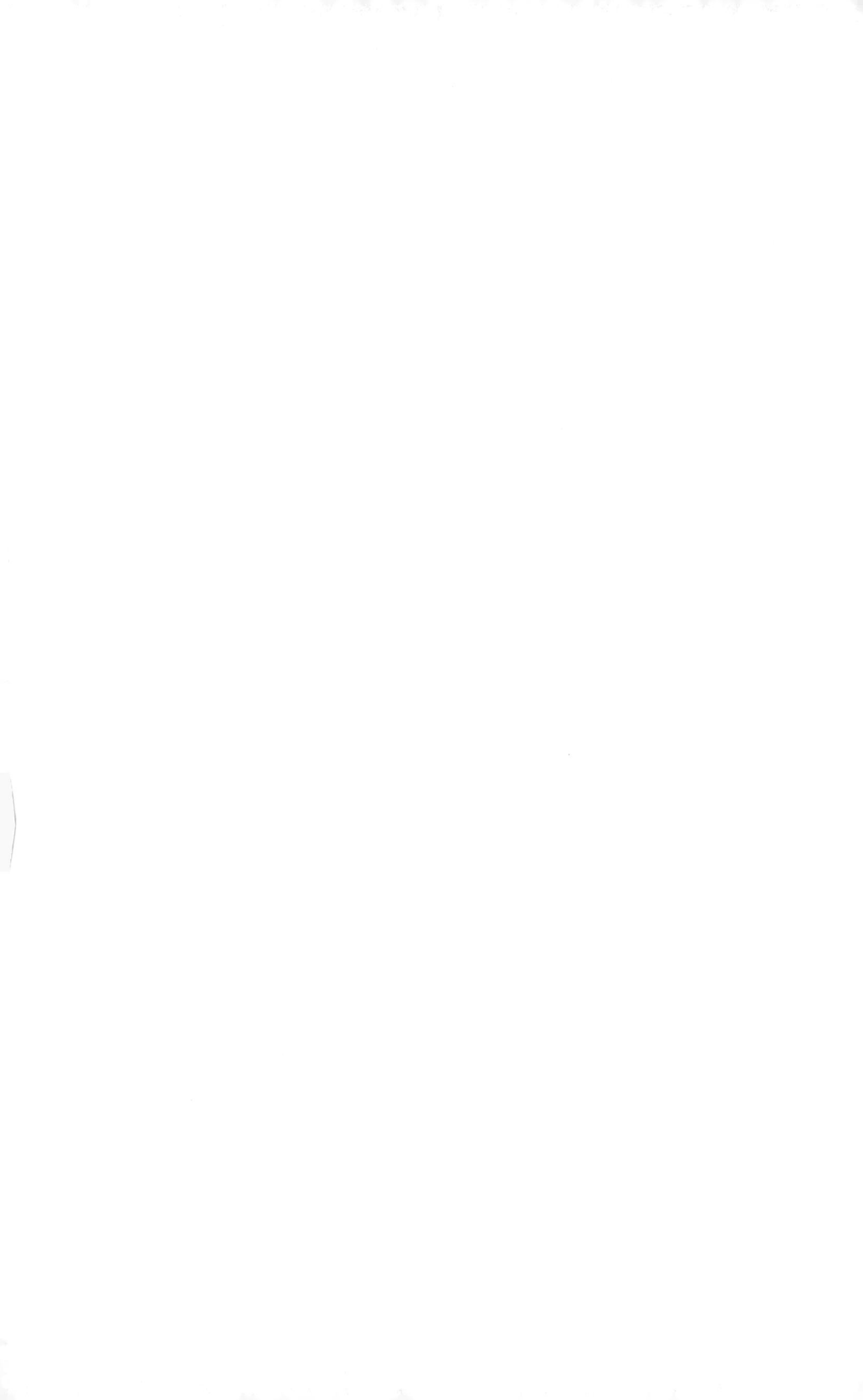